CW00553477

The
LAMBROOK
LEGACY
— 1860 ✳ 1997 —
A HISTORY OF LAMBROOK SCHOOL

From Starched Collars
to Sweatshirts

LAMBROOK IN 1880
The lake was drained in 1911.

THE LAMBROOK LEGACY

—— 1860 ✶ 1997 ——

A History of Lambrook School
from starched collars to sweatshirts

ISLA BROWNLESS

WITH A FOREWORD BY
MAJOR GENERAL
SIR ROY REDGRAVE KBE, MC

EVERGREEN GRAPHICS
CRAIGWEIL ON SEA
ALDWICK

THE LAMBROOK LEGACY 1860–1997

Lambrook Haileybury School
Winkfield Row, Bracknell
Berkshire RG42 6LU

WATERCOLOUR BY EDWARD DOWDEN 1991

First published in 1997 by
EverGreen Graphics
Kufri, 11 The Drive, Craigweil On Sea
Aldwick, West Sussex PO21 4DU

ISBN 1 900192 01 2

Designed by Cecil Smith
Typeset by EverGreen Graphics
Craigweil On Sea, Aldwick, West Sussex PO21 4DU

Printed and bound in the United Kingdom by
Redwood Books Ltd
Kennet Way, Trowbridge, Wiltshire BA14 8RN

FOREWORD

BY MAJOR GENERAL SIR ROY REDGRAVE KBE, MC

IT HAS LONG BEEN FASHIONABLE to liken the time spent by boys at Preparatory Schools to something akin to banishment to a ghastly gulag for delinquent Peter Pans, but this book is a revelation, it is a vibrant and entertaining story about one of the oldest such institutions in Britain.

Through the playing fields there flows a gentle stream where boys have always carried out their bridging and hydro schemes. Throughout this narrative runs a strong thread of personal commitment and care by the teachers for their sometimes capricious and ever changing charges. Naturally new boys were terribly homesick, but the staff were sympathetic, boys were read to and sometimes allowed a whole day in bed being spoilt rotten, and teddy bears on the pillow.

There was never that feeling of fear which many boys experienced initially when faced with the harsher rules of a great Public School. At Lambrook boys thrived and soon gained self confidence. Quite imperceptible qualities of leadership were developed; boys became dormitory captains, wolf cub patrol leaders, feats of escape and evasion were attempted

Roy Redgrave and Adrian Clark in 1937.

playing Mouldy Line or French and English in the woods. So much for L'Entente Cordiale.

Good manners were encouraged, and even if they hated it, boys wrote a letter every Sunday. Boredom was never allowed to persist for too long and even the obligatory Sunday walks became nature rambles or an occasion for story telling. In this way the staff got an afternoon off, but somebody had to take the walk. To their eternal credit teachers never allowed the boys to know their frustrations or problems. Did they keep a bottle of Tio Pepe in the Common Room? Did they slip down to the pub to drown their sorrows? How did they ever manage on their salaries to carry out a courtship? This book has some of the answers.

To small boys arriving at Lambrook the sheer size of everything was awesome. As they grew older things diminished until years later only the invisible remains a cherished memory. Those whose parents lived abroad were able to benefit from the keen interest taken in them and the security of a second base. Some remember the sounds of Lambrook; cheers as a bus with a victorious football team returned up the drive, the chime of the school clock, the rare clunk of a cricket ball against the pavilion, the riotous singsong at the end of term. Let us also include a memorable silence when the boy working the bellows behind the organ fell asleep during a singularly dull sermon. Now there is a little electric switch.

This book charts the course of a resourceful school past innumerable pitfalls which would have finished lesser establishments. But it had a sense of purpose, an excellent record, a highly professional staff, and above all a great sense of fun.

ROY REDGRAVE

November 1997

MOULDY
LINE
IN THE
1930s

CONTENTS

LIST OF ILLUSTRATIONS

PREFACE

"You can't draw every leaf on the tree"

I NOW APPRECIATE the significance of the art teacher's remark to my father. If the tree is fine and large, in a wonderful setting, one should stand back: looking at it in close up, one sees innumerable small beauties and delights.

Lambrook, like its oak trees, is impossible for me to view dispassionately. My position as daughter, wife and mother of three men who have nursed Lambrook through near-death experiences has given me a unique view. To these three this book is dedicated.

My thanks are also due to innumerable people who have helped. I have gratefully acknowledged many in the text but some I thought would prefer anonymity. I should like to have acknowledged hundreds of other 'leaves' who have been part of this fine tree.

Blaming other people for shortcomings is always tempting but with the three generations looking over my shoulder, I must own up: the mistakes and omissions are mine alone.

Looking back can help one look forward: Lambrook now embarks on a new era. Merged with Haileybury Junior School, it has the opportunity to serve more generations. A different emphasis, more day children than boarders, can give wider influence in the locality. The scope for service and fun will be different but greater. The combined school, once such difficulties as what to shout by way of touchline encouragement have been resolved, begins its new life with the high hopes and best wishes of the past.

The Hornpipe   ISLA BROWNLESS
Oak Meadow   NEE FORBES
Birdham
Chichester   *November 1997*
West Sussex
PO20 7BH

A DIGRESSION
ON NAMES

OURS IS A CONFUSING CENTURY: the way we address or refer to each other changes constantly. This book covers 137 years, has a large cast and many of them were referred to differently at different times. There is scope for confusion.

I have avoided initials as too often confusing in themselves: AEF, AHF and EFF were three people whose initials are too alike. Mr. Johns is the exception. He was addressed for 23 years as RVJ or Mr. Johns though everyone referred to him affectionately as Daddy Johns. He was cautious about his Christian name and the nickname from his schooldays was a close secret.

Christian names alone tend to confusion as there are not enough of them: I should be sorry if anyone mixed up Philip Squarey and Philip Brownless. Fortunately Phil Squarey was seldom given his whole name. The exceptions are those people whose names recur. Archie Forbes spent 42 years at Lambrook, addressed as Forbes in his schooldays and among older colleagues even into the '50s. I have stuck to Archie throughout. My mother was widely called Flora but when she grew older than current parents, Mrs.Forbes became a term of affectionate respect. It feels wrong to refer to the Rev.F.D. Browne as anything but Mr.Browne because he was always addressed thus when he was old and I was young.

Boys gave nicknames to each other and to masters, though they addressed them as Sir and hoped the nicknames were unknown. I was called Carthorse till Philip became widely known as Burma (behind his back, of course) and then I was promoted (?) to Ma Burma. These secrets did not last long as shouting is easier for boys than whispering.

An Old Boy can be worried lest his own nickname gets stuck to his son. I have known of two in quite a state about this: one swore my father to eternal secrecy and later another took me aside and exacted the same promise. Many nicknames are affectionate and become so widely used that a boy suspects trouble if he is addressed by his proper name.

I believe there are fewer nicknames today than fifty years ago: Christian names are used more often nowadays. In the far past boys were reticent about divulging Christian names even to each other. Surnames made a sort of protective covering, keeping school and home separate.

Reluctantly I have often resorted to using both names, though this can be ponderous, as in Cuthbert Norris Elye. Sadly I accept the charge of inconsistency but clarity has been my aim.

The Digressions in this book deal with single topics which seem to demand one gulp rather than sips throughout the otherwise chronological order of Lambrook's history.

I.H.B.

1

R. J. BURNSIDE
HEADMASTER
1860–1883

AS THE COUPLE DROVE THROUGH THE GATEWAY to their appointment with the Headmaster a small figure leapt out of the rhododendrons. The boy wore a pirate scarf round his head: he pointed his forefinger at them and said "B-b-b-bang". Then seeing they were visitors he dropped his weapon arm and removed his headscarf with a sweep, asking "May I help you ?"

This incident might have occurred at any time since Lambrook became a school in 1860. The essential boy has not changed though his dress, his speech, his lessons, his games are very different. This book consists largely of reminiscences from many different people. Although their recollections vary as widely as chalk and cheese and microchips, the connecting threads of place and time seem to highlight the similarities rather than the differences between them.

"Lambrook was smaller then," wrote one who was at school there in the 1860s, "although the boys were larger, older, probably more stupid, and consequently more inflated with pudding and a sense of their own importance.

"We learned to swim in an open bath at the bottom of the playing fields. It was beastly cold in almost any weather. Not many of us cared about the bathing, although we would never have admitted any fault so un English. There was a very fat boy, since either dead or a marquis, whose dislike of the chilly water made him especially careful of plunging in. It was his habit to test the water in a peculiar manner. He pushed us in first and judged by our colour. If we turned blue he stopped on the bank. If we turned lobster red he would paddle in the shallow end, whereas if we remained our natural hue he might be tempted to steep his royal fatness in the deeper places.

"We played very little football or cricket and had no matches at all. We indulged in rounders and games with knotted handkerchiefs – very painful games they were – and we fought a good deal. I once fought a most bloodthirsty battle with a certain nobleman who had scored the same number of marks as myself for the drawing prize. We decided, or it was decided for us, to fight. The battle lasted a long time, perhaps twenty minutes, and was brought to a lame conclusion by the inconvenient arrival of a master. My

MR. AND MRS. ROBERT BURNSIDE 1877
at the front door of Lambrook in their pony phaeton

reward was 100 lines, a melancholy interview with the Headmaster and the drawing prize."

This Old Boy looked back "with love and reverence for the grey walls and glad associations of his preparatory school days." Herbert Asquith, another Old Boy, expressed the opposite view: "I have never met anyone who looked back with enthusiasm to his life at a private school and in this I am no exception."

Ernest Sykes,who left Lambrook in 1880 wrote "Cricket was the real school game and a little football in the winter. Also long walks. We slept in small dormitories (about four in each room) in the top of the main house. There was a shop opposite called Omans where we spent our money and there was a small pond in front where we skated one winter for a long time."

How did it begin as a school? What was there before that? How old is the cedar tree? Why is the drive so wide and the gateway so narrow? How long has the stream been called The Lamb?

The name Lambrook occurs in the Court Rolls of Wynkefyld Manor in 1440 when one John Bowyer was granted the tenure of a "croft of bond arable land called Lambrokes in Wynkfyld." Then there is silence for 400 years.

In 1853 William Budd built the house with an impressive front and terrace, a fine staircase, library, conservatory and spacious rooms. He laid out gardens with a lake, shrubberies and drives and planted the cedar trees. However, it was his for only seven years.

Robert J.Burnside had tutored boys in his house at Blackheath and moved to Lambrook in 1860 with an eye to the court at Windsor. Public schools then accepted boys at widely varied ages and *Tom Brown's Schooldays* published in 1857 highlighted the abuses of a system in which

LAMBROOK'S FIRST SCHOOL GROUP 1879

The headmaster in the middle is Mr. R.J. Burnside. The other master is Mr. Soulser. On Mr. Burnside's right is Prince Christian Victor; on his left Drumlarig and next to him is Prince Albert Victor. The boy in the basket chair is Lord Ancaster and on his right is E.R. Sykes (who sent the photograph.) Among the rest are Hencaye, Pelhams, Moor, Ferguson and Gilliat.

POST OFFICE TELEGRAM

From Balmoral to Mr Burnside 27 August 1878. "The Queen wishes you to bring Prince Christian Victor of Schleswig Holstein here tomorrow for luncheon at two o'clock. Please let me hear you are coming."

boys of ten or younger struggled for survival in a regime geared for 18 year olds. Many preparatory schools came into being in the 1860s. Lambrook is one of the few with an unbroken history in the same buildings.

The only master then was the bearded Mr. Soulser. He must have been versatile as he taught whichever subjects or boys the headmaster did not want to teach. The first Lambrook school photograph in 1879 shows Mr. Soulser and 21 boys in a variety of suits and high buttoned waistcoats grouped around the headmaster who wears a curly brimmed bowler hat. The impression is of a lively group finding it difficult to stay still for the required three and a half minutes. E.R.Sykes gave this photograph to the school. He is seated next to Prince Christian Victor who – though his grandmother might not have been amused – was known as Eggy to his friends.

RJB's scrapbook of newspaper cuttings offers glimpses of a 'dramatic entertainment' at Lambrook and a burglary foiled by Miss Burnside as well as lists of candidates successful in the army examination, doubtless Old Boys whose careers RJB was following. The Court Journal of 1875 records that "the Earl of Yarborough, the Hon.C.Finch and Mr. and Miss Burnside left the Mills of Cairn, Ballater, where they have been staying for the last month, for Lambrook, Berkshire."

St. Ronan's, the house next door to Westfield, was owned by the Misses Manners, whose niece became Mrs. Burnside. Five of their seven children were born at Lambrook. A photograph in 1877 of Mr. and Mrs. Burnside in a splendid pony phaeton by the front door shows a dashing dark haired man with side-burns. A few years later he appears a slightly stooped paterfamilias, standing with his children and dog on the front steps.

The Court Circular from Balmoral in 1878 noted that "Her Majesty's grandson, Prince Christian Victor of Schleswig Holstein, who is staying at Braemar lunched with the Queen and Royal Family. Mr. Burnside who accompanied the young Prince had the honour of being pre-sented to Her Majesty." By now these two grandsons of Queen Victoria were at Lambrook and their headmas-ter evidently tutored them in the summer holidays as well.

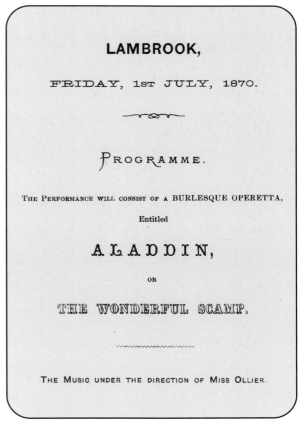

LAMBROOK,

FRIDAY, 1st JULY, 1870.

PROGRAMME.

THE PERFORMANCE WILL CONSIST OF A BURLESQUE OPERETTA,

Entitled

ALADDIN,

OR

THE WONDERFUL SCAMP.

THE MUSIC UNDER THE DIRECTION OF MISS OLLIER.

Legend has it that Queen Victoria had tea at Lambrook from a fine china tea service with a dark blue pattern. The last cup and saucer were treasured by younger Burnsides a century later. Old villagers certainly remembered Queen Victoria driving in a landau along Cricketers Lane and stopping with her escort of house-hold cavalry to watch the cricket.

At Christmas 1879 the same burlesque *Aladdin* was repeated. This time Prince Christian Victor was the 'Genius' of the Ring and the cast included two imps, Prince Albert and Mr. John Manners. There were 40

Characters.

The Sultan (*a Monarch in difficulties, and anything but a Rex pecuniarum*) .... Mr. NIGEL KINGSCOTE.

The Vizier (*who amidst other dirty work, is supposed to have cleaned out the Exchequer*) .... Mr. ROBERT GIFFORD.

Pekoe (*the Vizier's hope and his own pride*) .... Mr. ARTHUR LAYARD.

Aladdin (*an anomaly, for, although he is considered by every one to be a " lively youth," he is universally looked upon as a " sad boy"*) .... Mr. ARTHUR TRITTON.

Abanazar (*a Magician who has been round the world in search of the lamp, but who finds great difficulty in getting round Aladdin*) .... Mr. HENRY GIFFORD.

Te-to-tum (*an Attendant*)................................. Mr. GUNNING KEEN.

The Slave of the Lamp .... LORD BURGHERSH.

The Genius of the Ring .... Mr. ARTHUR BURNSIDE.

The Widow Twankay (*Aladdin's mother, "who" to quote the Arabian Nights, "was rather old, and who, even in her youth, had not possessed any beauty ?"*) .... Mr. ARTHUR BURR.

Princess Badroulboudour (*" This Princess was, in fact, the most beautiful brunette that ever was seen: her eyes were large, well placed, and full of fire," &c.—Arabian Nights.*) .... Mr. RAYMOND LAYARD.

Maidens, Mandarins, and Mob.

SCENERY, INCIDENTS, &C.

SCENE I.—"*Hand-tea*" ROOM IN THE SULTAN'S PALACE.

The Skipper and his boy.—How the Sultan catches the Vizier upon the hop, and how the Vizier has the Sultan upon the hip—A modest proposition, and a bold resolution.

SCENE II.—A STREET IN PEKIN.

Arrival of a mysterious Wizard-er from the south—How Aladdin affronts the stranger, and how he is himself taken aback—How the long-lost brother is found short—How he is looked upon as an impostor, but how he is believed to be innocent, when he discloses his gilt.

ALADDIN
OR THE WONDERFUL SCAMP
A Burlesque Operetta performed at LAMBROOK
on Friday 1st July 1870
The music under the direction of Miss Ollier.

Scene III.—THE JEWELLED CAVERN.

How Aladdin goes in by himself, but falls out with Abanazar—How he receives a ring, accompanied by a knock, and how Abanazar goes right off, his ring being left on. The Lamp! The Ring! The Rub!

THE GENIUS OF THE RING.

Scene IV.—ALADDIN'S COTTAGE.

How Aladdin looks out of wind-oh, and how his Mother almost loses her breath.

THE SLAVE OF THE LAMP.

A magic meal.—Oh, Gem-ini!—How the Widow carries Aladdin's proposition for the Princess's hand.

Scene V.—IN THE SULTAN'S PALACE.

A slow match, and eventual blow up.—How the Widow is introduced at Court, and makes a decided impression.—Extraordinary change for a sovereign.—Terrible riot at the Union, and opportune arrival of out-door relief.—Expression of delight at prospects of existence in an attic on the upper story, and expression of indignation to an upper-attic finale.

Scene VI.—EXTERIOR OF ALADDIN'S PALACE.

Buy! buy! buy! Any new lamps for old ones?—How the Princess gets into trouble, and is transported in *jew seizing.*—How the Princess is carried off.—and how the Sultan and Widow carry on.—How Aladdin finds his friend stick to him, though his pal-has gone to Africa!

Scene VII.—SALOON IN THE MAGIC PALACE.

How the Princess rejects Abanazar's name and numerous addresses.—How he plays his cards badly, and though a good hand at twist, finds he has lost the rub.—How the lamp changes owners.—How the four intruders run him through as a fore-runner to what is to follow.—How the house literally "comes down," followed by the curtain, and it is hoped the applause of a

GENEROUS BRITISH PUBLIC.

Manager   -   -   -   Mr. R. CATHCART.

Scenery and Costumes by Messrs. J. SIMMONS & SONS, 4 Tavistock Street, W.C.

guests and the critic wrote a rave review, with an eye no doubt on the royalty in the cast and the audience.

In 1883 Mr. Burnside left Lambrook and went to live in France. He was presented with an illuminated scroll and a purse containing £100 "in appreciation of the untiring energy and kindness which you have so invariably shown in your long and arduous career."

A DIGRESSION ON
THE LAUNDRY

THE LAUNDRY WAS ABOUT NINETY YEARS OLD when it was pulled down in 1978 to make room for the squash court. It was a single storey building covered with green painted corrugated iron. All the school laundry was done here in Mr. Mansfield's time "and probably saved our parents quite a lot of money" according to Audley Gray.

In the first room, the washing was done in a fog of steam at huge wooden sinks under the west window. An expert laundress and three maids did everything, boys' clothes, bed linen and towels, the long damask table cloths for the dining hall, the boys' white table napkins as well as the choir surplices. Blankets and curtains were washed in the holidays.

The water was heated in a vast copper (the gardeners lit the fire at dawn) and the maids carried the hot water to the sinks in galvanised buckets and bailers. They used great bars of yellow soap and rubbed the clothes on washboards. The stone floor ran with water which was swept into drains under the sinks and the maids stood on duckboards to work. On wash days they wore big sacking aprons over their green overalls. The indoor maids wore caps but the laundry maids worked bareheaded and all the clips and combs and kirbygrips in the world could not restrain their hair. When the outside door opened, it was like a ballet movement – backs straightened, heads turned and wet red arms were raised in unison to wipe back the straggling hair before they smiled in greeting through the steam.

The wet clothes were roughly folded and then fed through the mangle (two wooden rollers turned by a handle on a heavy wheel) to squeeze out most of the water. Two maids did this heavy job together and then the wet things were carried out in huge baskets to be hung on wires in the drying ground between the laundry and the six fir trees.

The inner room of the laundry was the ironing room. It was immensely high with overhead racks and pulleys and half a dozen extra tall clothes horses. Rows of flat irons in three sizes, thirty in all, were ranged in a pyramid round the Tortoise stove. A high wooden ironing table, padded with old blanket and covered with sheeting, ran along the south side beneath the windows and the maids chatted to people passing outside. There were pin up pictures and in the 1930s, Prince Charming, soon to become King Edward VIII, held pride of place.

Ironing was an energetic business: each maid had three irons on the go, one in use and two heating. Fifty years later, one of these laundry maids picked up a flat iron in a junk shop and was amazed that as girls their wrists were strong enough to turn over the heavy size 12s. They trotted to and from the stove holding the hot irons with pads of rag. They wiped the iron soles clean of coal dust before spitting on them or holding them up near their cheeks to test the temperature. Then they tackled the clean linen lying ready in long dampened rolls like school suet puddings. Special things like the choir ruffs, done with a tall goffering iron, narrow enough to get right into pleats and gathers, became a work of art. The Tortoise stove glowed red hot and aired everything hanging high up in the roof.

The washing room was a scene of intense activity: the ironing room was more relaxed with a faint smell of scorching, and laughter and cups of tea. To the maids the work must often have seemed endless but one who came from an orphanage aged 16 said fifty years later that Lambrook had been a good home and a family to her and she was grateful for the companionship and the chance to learn these skills.

In the 1930s the Lambrook Electrical Club (three boys who were good with electrics and had the gift of the gab) fixed up loudspeakers in the laundry and from the touchline relayed running commentaries of matches.

Miss Nicholls presided over the laundry for 28 years, retiring in 1939. Vera Peach and another girl went off to do war work and Laura got married, returning later to work in the laundry singlehanded. Some of the school laundry was sent out but she coped with prodigious quantities of work by hand until she retired in 1958 after 39 years.

Laura bicycled from Goose Corner in every weather and her progress up the hummocks of the long field, wobbling slowly through the muddy or snowy grass, was watched from many windows. Only once was she seen to get off her bike and push it up the last bit. She arrived on the tick of 9 a.m. and if a new gardener had not lit the fire beneath the copper early enough, her wrath was awe inspiring. Strong men trembled and assistant matrons fled in terror.

Her cigarette stayed on her lip by itself and she could shake ash off it with a toss of her head as her hands were always busy. Arms deep in suds, she scrubbed away at some garment reviling the newfangled washing machines which came into use in the 1950s. "Never mind", she would say as she tackled 100 vests, 100 pairs of pants, 100 pairs of stockings and 100 shirts by hand, "I'll soon have them right again."

When the Tortoise stove finally collapsed and an electric iron had to be bought, the Headmaster was called in to

FLAT IRONS

heating on the Tortoise Stove in the Laundry.

break the news to Laura, in such awe was she held by all. She took it calmly though, simply saying that she had an electric iron at home now.

Today there are washing machines indoors and the assistant matrons deal with some of the boys' laundry. Although easy care fabrics have lightened the work another chore has arisen – the endless checking of lists and phone calls to the outside laundry. Keeping Lambrook cleanly clothed has never been easy.

2

E.D.MANSFIELD
HEADMASTER
1883–1904

Author's Note: For this section I am greatly indebted to Audley Gray, the eldest of five brothers who all came to Lambrook and enjoyed it. With two of his brothers he visited the school for the first time sixty years after leaving and their recollections were so vivid I begged him to write them down. Some weeks later he sent me a long article entitled LAMBROOK IN 1900. I have discussed this with others who knew Lambrook then. Another contemporary record is from W.F.Bushell, at Lambrook from 1895 to 1898, who became headmaster of Birkenhead School. Audley Gray also taught, so both men wrote knowing how schools had changed in their life time. The changes have been even greater since. Aspects of past Lambrook seem barbaric to us in the 1990s but Old Boys a century ago appear to have recorded them simply as poor parts of a good whole.

THE MAN AND HIS PLAN

L EGEND HAS IT THAT LAMBROOK had run down somewhat at the end of R.J. Burnside's time. Most likely there were money troubles as parents with noble names were sometimes ignoble payers. It seems the number of boys dropped suddenly: Arthur Watson Smith was "one of the original 12 boys in 1883" but E.D.Mansfield's book of form lists shows 41 boys in 1884 and there were 46 boys in the school photograph in 1885 so the school expanded briskly.

Edward Dillon Mansfield was 39 when he came to Lambrook. He had taught classics at Clifton College and was headmaster for nine years of their new preparatory department. Six testimonials to him, in a booklet printed in 1883, make astonishing reading as he appeared to have every virtue, being "completely adapted for educating boys." The headmaster of Hillbrow thought him "perfect as a gentleman, perfect as a teacher, perfect as an educator in the wider sense." A colleague added "I am aware that what I have written is very strong but it is written with measured deliberation, representing my impartial judgement and, if it errs, does so on the side of understatement." The headmaster of Clifton and his predecessor backed their glowing testimonials by sending their sons to Lambrook.

He was three times chairman of the Association of Headmasters of Preparatory Schools, formed in 1892. Concerned about wide variations in the entrance requirements of public schools and the over full curriculum of preparatory schools, E.D.Mansfield worked towards a common entrance examination (achieved in 1904), a training scheme for assistant masters (set up in 1897) and a more widely based curriculum. He wanted fewer hours spent on Greek and more on English, history and geography as well as nature study and manual skills. He wrote Latin and Greek text books and a paper on teaching with the perceptive words "The memories of young boys are like nets, full of holes."

Their memories may have been like nets but several boys of this time trawled up lively recollections. W.F.Bushell, later a headmaster, left in 1898. "It would be easy to exaggerate and to represent our life as one of continual excitement; to dilate on all kinds of horrors and sufferings, especially as every generation likes to tell their successors what a happy and comfortable life they live compared to the past. No doubt this is generally true... but it becomes a wearisome platitude and I should imagine it must be less true of Lambrook than of most schools. The Lambrook of 1895 must have been well up to the standard of the day if not above it." As an example he cited the little changing room with three basins (known to later generations as The Bibble) for washing after games: he thought this "luxurious" as his well known public school had no baths for boys' use until his last year.

The school fees were £40 per term in 1900: the Gray parents thought this a high fee but good value for the excellent teaching, excellent food, very good lecturers etc. There were few extras: medical attention was the only one of significance.

Audley Gray said E.D.Mansfield was "a recognised authority on education, in many ways in advance of his times. His reputation was such that we were visited by deputations from foreign governments to see how an English prep school was organised. As a result, the French government started a school, Les Roches, modelled on Lambrook."

When E.D.Mansfield retired after 20 years as headmaster of Lambrook, he served on Berkshire's Education Committee, on the Council of Reading University, and was a governor of several local secondary schools. He died in 1924 aged 79.

What was he like? Cuthbert Norris Elye, who later came to Lambrook, was his godson and was delighted on his seventh birthday to be presented by his godfather with a "magic matchbox" and even more delighted to find it contained half a sovereign. Arthur Watson Smith, at Lambrook in the 1890s, said EDM was "a far better teacher than any who taught me afterwards at Charterhouse."

E.D.Mansfield, usually called Teedy by the boys, according to Audley Gray, "was definitely awe inspiring. We can't be said to have had affection for him but we had the deepest respect. Though stern, he was absolutely fair – he never showed favouritism and we dimly appreciated the fact that he was a first class teacher. Teedy was ready to adopt new ideas but he never forgot that the essential thing was to get the boys to learn how to work. Stupid boys were not expected to get to the top of their form but a slacker got short shrift."

On Sunday evenings the whole school had milk and biscuits in the dining room. "It was a dreaded meal for Teedy held an inquisition into the crimes and misdemeanours of the past week. As no one's conscience was completely clear, each boy felt he might be the culprit to bear the brunt of the storm. As we timidly munched our biscuits, our eyes were on Teedy all the time. He strode up and down with a frown on his face and if the offence was a heinous one he would gnaw the ends of his moustache – this was a danger signal, like the swishing of his tail by an angry lion. Afterwards we trooped up to bed in a subdued frame of mind, particularly the boys who were due for a caning the next morning."

Cecil Green, a lifelong resident of Winkfield Row, told me about his early days when Mr. Mansfield, for years a Parish Councillor and one of the school managers, was a familiar and respected figure in the village. Cecil Green was at the Winkfield Row School where Mr. Tipper was headmaster, and "only allowed to hit our hands". If a boy did something very naughty – and eighty years later Cecil was not divulging what he had done – then one of the school managers was sent for to administer the cane. E.D.Mansfield lived nearest. He had a black walking stick with a silver knob which unscrewed to reveal a swishy cane inside. Cecil said "Mr. Mansfield was a fine big man and wore a Norfolk jacket. The girls were sent out of the room while we were caned. It didn't hurt much."

When Mrs. Mansfield came to Lambrook in 1890 as a bride of 18, her brother, later Brigadier Ross, came as a new boy aged eight. (The usual age of entry was ten.) The Mansfields' two sons were in the school and sixty years later Geoffrey Mansfield was a regular visitor when his grandson Peter came to Lambrook. Mrs. Mansfield was a "somewhat dim and shadowy figure to the boys" said Audley Gray. "We naturally thought of her as an elderly woman. (She was 28 in 1900.) She ran the domestic side of the school, for there was no housekeeper, and she must have done it well but she certainly didn't hold the vital position in the school that most headmasters' wives do today.

"After dinner one day Teedy announced that his wife was giving a prize to the boy with the cleanest hands and fingernails. The examination took place at once so that no competitor could slip away to do the necessary. We thought this a peculiarly feminine competition and no one minded losing. Another incident was rather odd. One night when we were dropping off to sleep, she came into our dormitory in evening dress and gave each of us a large handful of Fullers' best mixed sweets. This was a delightful gesture which we appreciated though we couldn't understand it. Later it came to our ears that Teedy was very angry about it."

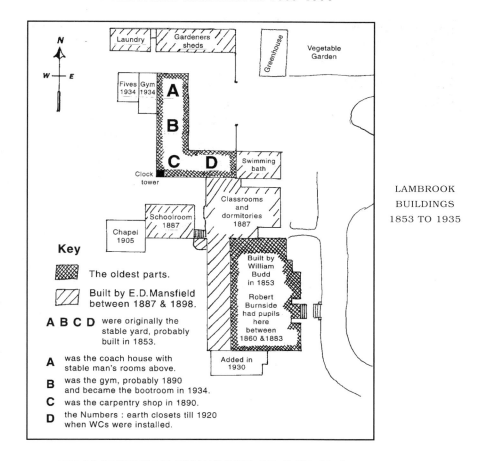

LAMBROOK BUILDINGS 1853 TO 1935

Laundry

Gardeners sheds

Greenhouse

Vegetable Garden

N

W — E

Fives 1934 | Gym 1934

A

B

C **D**

Clock tower

Swimming bath

Classrooms and dormitories 1887

Schoolroom 1887

Chapel 1905

Built by William Budd in 1853

Robert Burnside had pupils here between 1860 & 1883

Added in 1930

Key

The oldest parts.

Built by E.D.Mansfield between 1887 & 1898.

A B C D were originally the stable yard, probably built in 1853.

A was the coach house with stable man's rooms above.

B was the gym, probably 1890 and became the bootroom in 1934.

C was the carpentry shop in 1890.

D the Numbers : earth closets till 1920 when WCs were installed.

AN AMBITIOUS BUILDING PROGRAMME

The site of Lambrook was excellent but much building was needed. A four storey slice was added to the west side of the house. Some external walls became internal, and the outline of the triple arched windows can still be seen beneath the plaster. Another staircase was added, with metal treads to withstand the trampling hordes. A section of stairs under the grand front staircase was closed off as a cupboard with the treads as shelves.

Years later fire regulations caused this section to be reopened and a visitor called to see where she had been a maid sixty years earlier. She had run up and down the original stairs answering bells between her other tasks. Most rooms had a brass handle in a wall plaque connected to a double row of bells outside the kitchen. She said the people were nice but her mother took her away after a few months as the work proved too heavy for a 14 year old.

E.D.Mansfield built the classroom block beside the house. "Unlike

1888

E.D. Mansfield built the classroom block on the right. Lambrook looked like this till 1966 when a new floor was added to the classroom block making it the same height as the house.

most schools Lambrook was lit by electricity" according to Audley Gray. "It was generated by a surly electrician in a mysterious building in the yard. Also we had central heating in some parts of the building, an unusual luxury."

By 1888 the schoolroom had been built: it had an organ and was used for Sunday evening services. In 1892 Arthur Asquith wrote to his father who was Home Secretary "They are making the organ with carved pillars of wood." A century later the schoolroom was described as a 'temporary structure of brick and beam'. Nevertheless it has accommodated concerts, assemblies, lectures, debates, magic lantern shows and films, boxing and gym competitions, a model steam engine rally and parties of all sorts. In 1972 it was widened to become the present dining hall – not a bad century's work for a temporary building.

A heated indoor swimming bath was built and used all the year round. The water was changed about twice a term "when it had become a deep green colour." Then Sergeant Major Butt spent a long morning scrubbing the slime off the walls with a stiff broom. "In the summer we had a quick plunge in the swimming bath before the first lesson at 7 a.m. running down from the dormitories in our nightgowns."

Orchard House was built in 1898. Schools often had a separate sanatorium so that infectious illness could be nursed well away from the main building. Orchard House was seldom used for this but most of the masters lived there, looked after by Mrs. Harbour whose husband was head gardener.

SCHOOLWORK

Audley Gray, later a school master, considered that more scholastic work was done in 1900 than today. "The hours worked were longer and so were the periods, none less than 50 minutes and mostly an hour. We started at 7 a.m. generally with a Latin lesson, and this went on till breakfast at 8 a.m. Work started again at 9 a.m. after prayers in the big schoolroom and went on till 11 when we had a break in the playground. We had two more periods in the morning and, except on half holidays, two more before tea. "Evening prep in the big schoolroom lasted 1 or 1½ hours. This work was taken seriously for a badly done exercise meant a long spell of extra work and more often than not a caning.

"Looking back I am surprised at how high the standard of work was, particularly in English and History. I remember reading several Shakespeare plays and the whole of Tennyson's "Idylls of the King" before I reached the top form. The top two forms learned Greek (Teedy gave a Greek New Testament to each of the leaving boys) and the Latin, from Mansfield's own book which was filled with cruel catches and traps, was thoroughly taught. The masters were demons at instilling the grammar and rightly so.

"Only French and maths in the higher flights were taught in sets: all other subjects were taught by one's form master. By the end of the day the boys had seen more than enough of him and vice versa. One advantage was the dovetailing of Latin and English. As the same man taught both subjects it was easier to understand English grammar and construction."

W.F. Bushell thought the teaching was thorough. "I came to school at the age of ten having already started Latin at seven, French at eight and Greek at nine. Indeed I always understood that at home (he was the youngest of six brothers) I was regarded as behind in not having started Latin till seven! I think we were generally rather proud to start it, as it implied something of dignity, associated with age and the coming of manhood."

Audley Gray remembered the 'beginner Greeks'. "Teedy took the top form in Latin before breakfast and three boys from the next form came in for elementary Greek. They sat together on a low bench in front of Teedy's desk and he always called them "Feather-bed", "Jelly-bag" and "Putty and Co." On Monday mornings he used to pare his nails with his pocket knife.

His skill in dealing with the nails of his right hand was so fascinating to watch that the budding Greek scholars found it difficult to concentrate on alpha, beta, gamma.

"There were 2 Scripture lessons per week. Teedy took the whole school together on Sunday mornings. I can see him now, dressed in a morning coat and striped trousers, standing before a large wall map of the ancient world and pointing out St. Paul's journeys with a billiard cue.

"The worst lesson of the week, dreaded by everyone, was the last on Saturday morning. A paper, graded for each form, was set on English parsing and analysis. Every boy found this an odious subject and a poor performance meant hours of detention while games were going on, and perhaps for most of the afternoon.

"Every boy had to learn some poetry every day except Sundays. This was done in prep in addition to other subjects. We started with simple stuff, perhaps only one verse, but it was graded up steeply so that the top form might do 10 lines of Ovid or 12 lines of Shakespeare. By the top form one's memorising powers were so well trained that the learning of "rep" (repetition) was taken in one's stride and presented no difficulty.

"You were given your task and you knew you had to do it or be punished and this often meant six strokes of the cane. The assistant masters were not allowed to use the stick but each had his own method of inflicting torture – 'horse bites', pinching cheeks, pulling hair etc. In theory it is difficult to defend these methods but in practice they were singularly effective." This regime ended when the Rev. F.D.Browne arrived in 1904.

THE MASTERS

"The fundamental difference between 1900 and now lay in the mutual attitude of staff and boys" wrote Audley Gray. "Today not only would the masters take a friendly interest in the boys and the boys quickly realise that the masters are there not just to teach them in class but to help them in various ways.

"With us it was entirely different. A wide gulf separated home and school and no boy cared to have any fusion of the two compartments. He would have been surprised and shocked if a master had referred in any way to his home life. We carried our reticence so far that even with other boys we tried not to divulge our Christian names and should have been covered with confusion if the names of our sisters had become known. Today's parents will have met most of the staff. In 1900 few fathers would ever have spoken with the men who were teaching their sons.

"We hardly regarded our masters as human beings and were strangely incurious about them. I don't suppose a single one of us ever wondered how these peculiar and rather disagreeable men spent their holidays. I well remember being astonished when I.G. Overton's mother arrived for a weekend, for I couldn't imagine that IGO had a mother".

"Fuscey Brown – a dark sinister looking man – wore pince nez and was a demon for sending boys up to be caned for poor work. We stood in a semicircle for oral work and if anyone made a bad mistake Fuscey would fling a heavy ebony ruler at his shins and he was not supposed to move out of the way. He was a good naturalist though and encouraged us in this."

The only master not disliked was "Tivvy" Tarver but Audley Gray was ashamed of how they treated him. "Steel filings, called Russian fleas, could be bought from the joke department of Gamages. When sprinkled on the bald pate of Tivvy Tarver as he corrected a Latin book, they set up such a violent irritation that the lesson came to an end.

"Mr.Stork was a tall athletic man, a "cricketing ace who slogged the ball over the trees". He was rapidly going bald though he must have been under 30. He taught the lower forms and was, I think, extremely lazy. His jaw, broken when he was at Cambridge, emitted a clicking sound which fascinated us."

"No one could forget Livingstone and his uncontrolled temper. He taught French and there was never a dull moment when he was about. An almost daily pastime was "baiting Livy" and when the cry was heard "There's a Livy bait on!" there was a mad rush to the scene to take part in this dangerous sport. It needed little provocation to make him foam at the mouth and it was then a case of 'sauve qui peut'. I have seen him cut a boy's head open by banging it against the sharp edge of a table and the surprise was that he didn't actually kill a boy. It is even more surprising that he was kept on the staff for so long.

"He taught French almost entirely orally. There were four large pictures of country scenes during the four seasons of the year. The questions were taken from a German text book in a repulsive mottled green binding and ditto the exact answers. After a stilted conversation about the denizens of the farmyard we used to end up singing French songs unaccompanied. This was sheer joy as it provided a golden opportunity for a Livy bait. After a few terms this jolly way of learning French had to be given up because of the deafening noise.

SCHOOL GAMES

"Rugger was played in the autumn term. Teedy disliked soccer and thought 60 – 65 boys the optimum number for a school as it provided two full games of rugger. IGO was responsible for the games and both he and Stork often played themselves, much to our discomfort and dislike.

"In the Easter term we played Shinty – a form of hockey – with formidable weapons like heavy crook handled walking sticks. In March we started serious training for sports which the staff liked but we definitely did not. We wore vests and running shorts and spiked running shoes. Casualties occurred when someone stepped on another's foot and we got very cold standing about. The actual day made up in part for what we had

LAMBROOK SCHOOL GROUP 1903

Mr. E.D. Mansfield and Mrs.Mansfield are in the middle : he has Pom on his knee and Jack, their younger son, sits at his feet. At the left is an unknown lady : next is Stork, then Miss Auckland and 'Fuscey' Brown next to E.D.M. Next to Mrs. Mansfield is 'Tivvy' Tarver, then Livingstone and I.G. Overton.

gone through, and though we were not in the least interested in the actual races we were thrilled by the magnificent prizes Teedy provided.

"In the summer term, there was cricket on four days a week and on the other days cricket practice nets, reserved for a few from the top game. Out of 60 boys I don't suppose more than 15 were considered worth coaching. On Saturday evenings baseball was played by the senior boys under IGO's instruction. It was explained to us that this was a superior and more manly game than rounders which was only fit for girls and small children."

W.F.Bushell, another boy of this time, regretted "that no one gave me any cricket hints; perhaps there were nets but I never used one, and never had any idea of the usual strokes. Boys were not then taught games as systematically as they are today. I remember my horror of Rugby football because I never knew what I was expected to do at critical moments and no one ever took the slightest trouble to explain."

This lack of coaching for interested youngsters is surprising in view of E.D.Mansfield's avowed intention of producing a rounded education. Perhaps the masters in white flannels and striped blazers lacked patience with beginners. This attitude changed when the new headmaster arrived.

MATCHES AND OTHER SCHOOLS

Audley Gray enjoyed matches against other schools. "The teams travelled in hay wagons drawn by two cart horses which seldom trotted. The boys sat on benches and the journey took so long that we often missed part of the morning's work and took picnic lunch. We sang school songs and must have presented a pleasing picture of innocent gaiety." There were virtually no houses then between Bracknell and Reading.

"The school we liked best was Cordwalles, very smart in their scarlet caps. Wixenford (where Ludgrove is now) was our most hated foe. Their headmaster and ours were too friendly to our way of thinking and set us the same exam papers so that each could boast to the other how well his boys had done. Mr. Arnold was always on our doorstep, having driven himself over in his carriage and pair. We thought him an eccentric monster because we believed he had married his god daughter ! This was probably quite untrue but it was regarded as so wicked that it was quite in keeping with our general opinion of the school.

"We also despised them because almost every boy had a handle to his name which revolted our democratic feelings. We regarded them as cissies (though they frequently beat us at rugger and cricket) because they had a sandpit and a swing in their grounds (would any self respecting prep school boy demean himself by playing in a sandpit?) We firmly believed that the boys were roused from their sleep every morning by the butler and footman who brought to each boy in bed a cup of coffee and a bun. This story remained current from year to year though of course there was no evidence whatever for its truth.

"The Dragon School was a more manly place under their famous head-master Mr. Lynam. No sandpit or early morning coffee for them. It was a much bigger school than Lambrook so a victory against them was worth two elsewhere. Our objection was to their disgusting professionalism. They were rewarded with cash on a definite scale – so much for 10 runs, so much for 20 and so much per wicket for the bowlers. Well and good if this had been done behind the scenes but not a bit of it – the pay was handed out on the cricket field and this displeased us because we were not given the same inducement to win.

TWO OUTINGS

"The Dragons were our most important rival at the Olympic sports meeting held at the end of the Easter term in Reading. This was attended by five schools and was the red letter day of the year for us.

"After breakfast, the Mansfields, the staff and the boys set off in farm carts to Bracknell station and after a short train journey we arrived in Reading about 10.30 a.m. Each boy was given half a crown and we were let loose to amuse ourselves. We made a beeline for sweetshops first and toy shops second. The streets seemed to be filled with boys window gazing, and all working their way through paper bags of sweets, nougat and Turkish delight holding first place.

"We assembled by the statue of Queen Victoria at 12.30, on time although few of us had watches. Horse drawn char-a-bancs took us to the county cricket ground where marquees had been put up, the largest to accommodate hundreds of us for lunch. After a grand meal and a short interval for digestion we took a somewhat tepid interest in the sporting events as it was a foregone conclusion that the Dragons would win. After prizegiving and tea came the leisurely journey back to Lambrook, all of us tired but happy.

"Considering how strictly Mr. Mansfield ran the school it was remarkable that he allowed the two top forms to go to Ascot races as a reward for good work. We walked the four miles there with a master on two of the four afternoons. After watching the royal party drive up the course we dispersed to wander over the heath. Far more interesting than the races were the gypsies, tipsters, cardsharpers and all sorts of riff raff. No misadventure befell any of us but what a broadminded man Teedy must have been. Most headmasters would be terrified to run the risks of that Ascot expedition.

CARPENTRY AND GYM

The carpentry shop was the long room under the clock, now the changing room. "Carpentry was another outstanding achievement" said Audley Gray. "Teedy took a great interest in this and we were taught by a genius at the job, a foxy looking man named Lawrence with a red pointed beard. The basis of Lawrence's teaching was that no nails or screws were to be used if the job could be done by dovetailing and it often took a year before a beginner's efforts came up to his standards. Beautiful articles were made, often with intricate veneers and inlays, and these were the genuine work of the boy carpenters and not the products of Lawrence's skill."

Each boy had his own set of tools marked with his initials, 3 chisels, 2 planes etc, kept in good order by Lawrence. One of the Gray brothers had his much used set sixty years later and Ronald Colles (1913-1917), also glad of Foxy's training, was still using his chisels in 1996.

Sergeant Major Butt came to Lambrook in 1891 from a crack cavalry regiment. "He always wore a black jacket and grey striped trousers and carried a short silver topped cherrywood stick under his arm. All the thousand and one jobs that are no one's specific duty fell to Butt" wrote Audley Gray, but his main duties were teaching swimming and gym. "I doubt whether any prep school had a higher standard of gymnastics than

Lambrook. Every form had 3 lessons a week, starting with dumb bell exercises. The dumb bells were made of lead with leather grips and were graded in weight. Fencing and single stick fighting had been given up shortly before I went to the school. Butt was a wonderful gymnast considering his age and the fact that he performed his feats of strength and agility dressed in his everyday clothes. We did the sort of gym that might be seen in the army gymnasium at Aldershot – long arm balances on the parallel bars and even "grand circles" on the horizontal bar. We had complete confidence in him."

The honours boards with the gymnasts' names are still in Butt's old gym, now the bootroom. All five of the Bentley brothers were good at gym, in fact it was the only thing about Lambrook which W.O.Bentley, the youngest, enjoyed. Perhaps his mind was already on cars.

DANCING CLASS

"On Tuesday evenings in the winter the whole school were taught dancing by Monsieur D'Egville, official dancing master to the Royal Family. His ancestors came to England as refugees from the French Revolution and each generation had produced at least one professor of dancing. Our man was a melancholy individual, tall and thin in a black frock coat, his scanty black hair parted in the middle and his yellowish face adorned with a silky drooping moustache. He never unbent, never smiled, and seemed to us extremely pompous and stilted.

"He arrived from London with a pianist and a bevy of doubtless charming young ladies to assist him. Preparing for the lesson was quite a business, hands and faces to be washed, hair to be brushed and parted, shining uncomfortable pumps to be fastened over the instep with elastic, and, worst horror of all, brown kid gloves which always seemed too tight.

"We paraded into the big schoolroom and had to bow to M. D'Egville who gave each of us a stately bow in return. The first part of the lesson was mastering the six positions of the feet. The dances were the usual children's ones of that period – waltz, polka, Highland Schottische, Lancers, Hornpipe etc. Every boy dreaded having to dance with one of the young ladies, and however ill matched one's partner was, we did our utmost to stick together through thick and thin.

"An air of profound solemnity brooded over the whole proceedings and lifted only at the end when we indulged in the Gallop. This must have been a great concession on D'Egville's part for no one as correct as he could possibly approve of such unrestrained abandon."

When Cuthbert Norris Elye was at Lambrook a few years later, dancing was taught by Madame Gautier. CLNE remembered her beads and necklaces and her perfume but nothing about the dancing at all.

FREE TIME

"In the summer term snob cricket was played with a cut down cricket bat and a tennis ball. Several games went on at once, the wickets being chalked against the gym wall. In the winter, the standard playground game in break was an exciting form of French and English. Neither inside nor outside were masters on duty during our free time and consequently there was a great deal of bullying.

"For senior boys who did not care for French and English, a pleasant alternative was to form a press gang, capture as many small boys as possible and shove them into the small shed by the schoolroom. About 30 footballs and all our cricket bats were kept here and the smell of oil was overpowering as there was no light or ventilation. In fact it made a splendid prison and was known as the Black Hole of Calcutta which it strongly resembled when it was crammed full of inoffensive small boys who were kept there until break ended.

"In the summer boys collected butterflies and there were many more about then. Fossils and geological specimens had a few patrons. There were also ardent collectors of birds' eggs, some bought surreptitiously from village boys at the gate behind the cricket pavilion. We were, of course, strictly forbidden to buy from them.

"Gardening was taken very seriously and there was keen competition for the plots. Gardening was not allowed on Sundays – how different from today! Prizes were given at the end of term for the best gardens.

"The naturalists, whose interest was fostered by Fuscey Brown, collected caterpillars and sometimes beetles. Each collector had a large box made in the workshop with perforated zinc forming one side and here the caterpillars worked out the cycle of their lives. Some boys suffered painful skin rashes from handling the furry specimens.

"Indoors we occupied ourselves much as the modern boy does with conkers, paper darts, and the usual games such as draughts and chess. There were a lot of chess players in the school, some of them quite good. Stamp collecting was probably more popular than today: nearly half the school were budding philatelists. Crests off envelopes were also collected for the parents of most of the boys used crested stationery."

"For some queer reason I collected farthings" wrote W.F. Bushell, "and after the Great War this hoard was found and an astonished bank official received a thousand farthings from the unimaginative relative who discovered them. Even a thousand farthings were worth little more than a pound: surely it would have been better to have preserved them and mused from time to time over the queerness of schoolboy collections? I have never heard of any other small boy who collected a thousand farthings though I suppose anyone could who desired to."

Audley Gray liked the marbles, "some of coloured stone but mostly of glass in different sizes. Many boys came back to school with a supply of marbles determined to win more. It was a simple game. A marble was placed on the floor and one's opponent rolled his marble towards it from about 12 feet away. If it hit, then both were his. The preliminary matching of the two marbles – to make sure they were of equivalent value – was the only part of the game which could lead to a dispute.

"I have never seen "Nibs" played except at Lambrook. It resembled the Victorian game of Spillikins. Fountain pens (stylos) were only just coming into use, quills for writing had disappeared except from banks, and steel nibs of every imaginable shape and size were almost universally used. The Waverley was the commonest and the J was popular. The Relief and the beautiful Silver Lady were superior and expensive. The game was played by two players on a table: after the two nibs had been matched for value the players took turns to flick their nib at their opponent's, the object being to slip under its point with the butt end of one's own. If one then struck the point of one's nib it threw the opponent's nib into the air and if it landed on its back it was forfeit. The game often lasted a long time and needed considerable delicacy of touch.

"We had no school library – each boy brought back books and by swopping one with another we got on very well. There were no comics: for light reading we had *Tit Bits*, *Chums* and *The Boys' Own Paper* and for more solid reading *The Strand*, *Windsor* and *C.B. Fry's* magazines. *The Strand* was the most popular: it serialised *The Hound of the Baskervilles* long before it appeared in book form.

BULLYING

"Life was full of interest and fun for most boys and Lambrook would have been a very happy school but for the bullying that went on though I suppose this was no worse than at other prep schools and it did condition us to the harsher experiences that most boys faced at their public schools.

"There was very little supervision, no masters prowling round combining in their persons the duties of a nanny, a policeman and an arbitrator. There were no official prefects. A boy was put in charge of each dormitory and took his responsibility seriously but that was as far as the monitor system went. "However, a practice had become established that the top form should make itself responsible for what went on. A wretched boy would be hauled up, put on trial and – if found guilty – beaten. The culprit was allowed to pick any member of the form to speak as his defending counsel and I must say that the boy so chosen generally did his best. When everything had been said, each member of the form wrote guilty or not guilty on a slip of paper and if guilty, how many strokes of the cane he should receive. This varied from one to four – not as you might think a single stroke of the cane but one from each boy so the *minimum* punishment was 11 blows.

"What brought this horrid system to an end was a particularly savage beating of 44 strokes given to a boy two days before term ended. On his first evening at home he was bathed by his grandmother who was quite properly horrified at the state of his "back". She wrote a furious letter to Teedy who of course knew nothing of what had happened. Full explanations were demanded and given when we got back to school and we were told that never again was the top form to take upon itself the functions of a court but any serious offence was to be reported to Teedy by the head of the school."

UPSTAIRS

"The matron was Mrs. Curley. She was not an educated person but she had the homely kindness of an old fashioned family nanny. She always dressed in black bombazine and frequently lost her steel rimmed spectacles. They were usually found pushed up on her forehead, hidden by her grey curls. If she saw a small boy looking out of sorts or unhappy she would take him to bed with her. I never had this privilege" wrote Audley Gray "but one of my brothers did." (This, by a kind elderly woman, might be misinterpreted today.)

"With the help of two maids, Mrs. Curley did all the matron's work and looked after our clothes. After tea each day the boys who had to have medicines came to her sitting room and dispensary at the bottom of the stairs. Her stock remedies were Scott's Emulsion, cod liver oil, castor oil, grey powders, and Parish's Food. This was a popular remedy. It was an iron tonic which had to be drunk through a long glass tube to prevent it blackening the teeth.

"We had hot baths twice a week, supervised by a dormitory maid whose task was to scrape our scalps with a sharp comb to prevent scurf – very painful. On other evenings we washed – each boy had his own basin – at washstands in the dormitory. Every night eucalyptus – to prevent colds – was burned in a small pan above a nightlight and gave off its protective fumes. The dim light was comforting to the nervous.

"Pyjamas had not been thought of in 1900. We wore cotton nightshirts and must have looked little angels. When Teedy caned a whole dormitory for ragging after lights out, they were a very unsatisfactory protection! Toothpaste was non existent: we used white or pink (carbolic) toothpowder but when Odol in a bottle made its appearance, we discovered that it made a stimulating liqueur, drunk neat or with a little water.

"Dr. Barron, dressed formally in a frock coat and top hat in which he kept his stethoscope, used to arrive in a carriage with a pair of horses. He regarded each of us as a private patient even when half the school was in bed in an epidemic and his fee was ten shillings per visit. Lambrook must have been a little goldmine for him – small wonder he could afford the grand carriage.

Teedy had a fox terrier called Pom who used to visit the dormitories and bite the boys' feet through the bedclothes. C.L.Norris Elye also remembered Teedie taking prayers in the dininghall one evening when Pom had a fit underneath the table. Both prayers and fit continued to their conclusions. For weeks afterwards the boys came eagerly to prayers hoping Pom would do it again.

CLOTHES

"On weekdays each boy wore what his fond mother thought suitable and some of the choices were not very clever" wrote Audley Gray. "Most wore knickerbocker suits, blue serge being quite common. The jackets were mostly Norfolk pattern, with plenty of pockets and a belt. The breeches fastened below the knee with a narrow buckled strap of material. The shorts ended with a three inch band of box cloth worn *outside* black stockings held up by elastic garters above the knee – " very inhibiting to the circulation".

"Black boots were worn by all except one Yorkshire boy who arrived new at half term wearing brown boots and brown gaiters.

"Soft collars had not been thought of: day in and day out we wore those horrible Eton collars. After a few launderings they developed a sharp ragged edge which cut into one's neck." Years later Old Boys used to raise their chins gingerly and run a finger round the back of their necks as they recalled the lasting impression made by these collars. Ties and caps were black and red, then the Lambrook colours.

"On Sundays there was a transformation for the 60 young gentlemen appeared in the complete Eton rig out which, poor dears, they had to wear all day. I don't suppose any jacket has ever been designed in such an unpractical way as the Eton jacket. It has every conceivable defect. We wore black silk cravats or large ties "made up" so that we were not faced with the problem of tying them. In addition to the Eton collar we all sported starched "dickies" and I am glad to think no modern boy can have any idea what those breastplates looked like.

"Dressed like this we marched in crocodile formation to Winkfield Church for morning service, wearing of course the regulation top hat. The very sight of us roused furious feelings of hatred in the hearts of the village boys who carried on a deadly feud against us.

"Teedy and Mrs. Mansfield conducted the procession to church, he looking very distinguished in the sort of rig you would see at Ascot today. The rest of the staff trailed along dressed in rather shabby tail coats but sporting expensive fancy waistcoats. On weekdays they all, Teedy included, wore Norfolk suits (Stork had worn his for 10 years when I arrived and was still wearing it four years later) with stockings to match, boots of course, and over their boots they wore very long spats made of box cloth which reached to the calf. This was the dress which a man out for a day's shooting or playing golf would have worn though on some links golfers still had to wear a scarlet jacket as a warning sign to passers by."

LAMBROOK,
BRACKNELL.

The hours are –
7.15. Morning Prayers.
7.20 – 8.5 School.
8.5. Breakfast –
9 – 11. School.
11 – 12. Break – (Gymnastic, workshop.de.)
12 – 1. School.
1.10. Dinner.
Afternoon school.
4.15 – 6 Tuesday & Thursday.
5 – 6. Monday & Friday.
None Wednesday & Saturday.
6. o'clock. Tea. (5.30 on half holidays)
Evening work
7 – 8. for little boys.
7 – 8.10 for elders.

The hours are -
7.15	Morning Prayers.
7.20-8.5	School.
8.5	Breakfast.
9-11	School.
Break.(Gymnastic, Workshop.L)	
12-1.	School.
1.10	Dinner.

Afternoon School.
4.15-6.	Tuesday & Thursday.
5-6.	Monday & Friday.
None	Wednesday & Saturday.
6 o'clock. Tea. (5.30 on half holidays)	

Evening Work
7-8.	for little boys.
7-8.10	for elders.
8.	Supper for juniors & bed.
8.10	Supper for seniors.
8.30.	Evening prayers.
9.	Lights out.

As to washing-
Every boy has a hot bath under the Matron's superintendence once a week, & also attends the Swimming Bath 3 or 4 times. In Summer a boy <u>can</u> have a Swimming Bath every day, & must have it at least 3 times a week.

I hope that your boy will make a happy start in school life & I have little doubt that he will do so from what you tell me about him.
    With Kind regards, I am

Yours sincerely
E.D.Mansfield.

FOOD

"Food is rightly one of the preoccupations in the minds of healthy boys" wrote Audley Gray. "My impression is that we were fed extraordinarily well at Lambrook in 1900. Breakfast always began with porridge, followed on Mondays by cold ham – I can see in my mind's eye those two lovely hams now – Tuesdays, hot grated ham on toast, Wednesdays, fried bacon, Thursdays, the finest pork sausages I have ever eaten, Fridays, fish, herrings, kippers etc, and Saturdays (the only poor breakfast) 2 oily sardines, Sundays boiled eggs.

    "The midday meal was again excellent, both the meat course and the sweet. Teedy and Mrs. Mansfield sat together at a small table: Teedy and IGO did the carving. The boys did not help with waiting for the supply of domestic servants was almost unlimited and very cheap.

    "By modern standards tea was quite inadequate. The management supplied only tea, bread and butter and jam, but we were allowed to bring back tuck in our playboxes – cakes, biscuits, potted meat etc. but when this was finished, no more was allowed from home except a birthday cake.

LETTER FROM THE HEADMASTER

Our final refreshment was milk and biscuits before going up to bed.

"We always had a grand Christmas supper of turkey and plum pudding at the end of the winter term and Lambrook must have been one of the few schools where goose was eaten on Michaelmas Day.

"On certain aspects of food Teedy was quite fanatical. We were not allowed any sweets nor any of the ordinary brands of chocolate, but twice a week each boy received a thick bar of Cadbury's Mexican chocolate, a pure variety which met with Teedy's approval. This was supplied gratis to us but I suppose our parents must have paid for it. There were a few hiding places in the building where sweets could be secreted but not many. Inside our leather hatboxes was an obvious place but even old Mrs. Curley was not too dim to be suspicious when a boy expressed a wish to go and *look* at his hat.

"To make up for the lack of sweets we were allowed to buy fruit, nuts etc. from a ragged and dirty old man known to us as L'Homme (actually Mr. Long) who trudged over from Windsor two or three times a week carrying a

L'HOMME

L'Homme sat between these two buttresses selling fruit to the boys. He carried a big basket and walked the 7 miles from Windsor and back twice a week for about 25 years, until 1919. After that A.E. Fernie or Archie Forbes bought sweets for the boys. They have called sweets "Shop" ever since the days of L'Homme.

large, heavy basket with enough in it to supply 60 boys at twopence a head.

"L'Homme used to take up his station between the brick buttresses of the schoolroom, with all the treasures neatly sorted into paper bags. Probably the best buys were dates and nuts of various kinds. Cherries are all right from a bag but strawberries most certainly are not. L'Homme was careful always to put one good strawberry on top of all the mingy ones: on his sale he probably made 200% but I think he fully earned it, poor man."

W.F. Bushell thought L'Homme was "rather a favourite with the boys and that his prices were reasonable. Today it would be easy to supply fruit as such a variety is imported but in 1895 it was not so: even the banana had hardly appeared. Melons were a great favourite: he cut off slices, covered them with sugar and we ate them greedily with our fingers. Probably apples and oranges were the staple fare." L'Homme was going strong twenty years later when Ronald Colles bought pomegranates from him and ate them in the dormitory, " trying to dispose of the rind by throwing it up the chimney and hoping it would lodge on a ledge."

Audley Gray recalled "an extraordinary incident to show how strongly Teedy felt about boys receiving food while in his care. Some parents had ordered 40 lbs of strawberries for the whole school. "Senior boys fetched them and we were thrilled at the thought of the unexpected treat. Then Teedy led the way into the kitchen garden where none of us had been before. We did think it an odd place for a picnic but that was not important, the strawberry feast was the thing. In the far corner we were startled to hear pigs grunting. (I expect they supplied the Monday hams.) There Teedy addressed us: it was a strict rule, he said, that no provender from outside should be consumed by the boys and though it was very kind of Mr and Mrs Blank, he could not allow us to have the strawberries. Each carrier in turn then had to come forward and tip the baskets into the troughs.

This was one of the major disappointments of my life. It was a shocking sight to see those greedy pigs fighting round the troughs, wolfing down strawberries with grunts of satisfaction, their snouts covered with red juice which looked like blood. Looking back, I think that was the most cruel thing Teedy did during my four years at the school."

Audley Gray refers with tantalising brevity to a dormitory feast held in a house in the village: "the only occasion in my life when I have eaten anchovies, Bombay duck, Harrods best wedding cake, soused herrings and tinned peaches in that order – I must have had the digestive powers of an ostrich and this must surely have been one of the greatest feats of organisation ever carried through by boys of our age."

Another memory remained vivid: "A fire broke out one afternoon in the sitting room shared by Stork and IGO. By the time it was noticed it had a good hold and as the nearest fire engine was at Bracknell – and it was horse drawn – there looked to be a good chance of our school going up in flames. Every boy was told to get something to hold water and a chain was formed to the swimming bath which was nearly emptied of water before the fire was put out. This was a very exciting afternoon."

These words, written when he was 73, convey a hint of the disappointment he felt as a boy when the fire was put out and the excitement over. However, he concluded *Lambrook in 1900* on a note of nostalgia: "There are only two short periods of my life that I would like to relive and one of them is my spell at the school. I hope that the present upholders of the fine Lambrook tradition, if they live to be old men, will be able to recall their schooldays with as much affection as I do mine."

A DIGRESSION ON
THE LAVATORIES

UNTIL 1919 THE LAVATORIES WERE EARTH CLOSETS. The heavy tubs were emptied each morning by the gardeners and the tradition lasted a further fifty years that lavatory cleaning was properly the work of the outside men. "The old earth closets" said one who used them, "had a box arrangement at the back. When you had finished you wobbled the seat and some earth fell down and covered it all neatly. No, it was not smelly."

They have been known as 'The Numbers' since time immemorial because of the small enamel figures on each door. A neighbouring school did not have doors to their cubicles and was despised by Lambrook boys on this account. When Mathematics became known nationally as Number, this name caused some concern to a nice minded master as it gave rise to sniggers quite unbefitting the seriousness of his subject.

The installation of the new water closets was approved by the London Sanitary Authority who inspected them annually (for a fee) and this was proudly stated in the prospectus until 1935 when at last the Winkfield Sewerage substation was built and the main drains came near enough for Lambrook to be connected. Then the rows of willow trees, almost an acre of them, growing on the Lambrook sewage field were pulled out to make the first game rugger ground.

The plumber's mate in 1919 was Mr. Alfred Harris, working with his father to put in the water closets. Fifty years later it was the same Alf Harris, now with his grandson as mate, who removed these same cisterns to install the new continuous flush cistern. Goodness knows how many cracked basins, worn out levers and plungers and burst pipes he has dealt with. He and members of his family have been familiar figures at Lambrook most of this century, occasionally coping with an emergency in term time but usually in the holidays working against time to complete some project before the heedless hordes returned to start pulling the plugs again.

During the big freeze up of 1962, in spite of Alf Harris's best endeavours, the school loos still did not work when the boys came back in January. Much telephoning took place and members of staff offered the appropriate "hospitality". A fearful rota was devised, P.T. was cancelled and after breakfast the boys dashed off across the snow, whooping joyously, in a dozen different directions to queue for loos in the masters' houses. Little did the neighbours know what they had narrowly escaped.

When the continuous flush cistern was installed (allowing plugs to be pulled with no delay for refilling) one boy, obviously a budding plumber, devised an ingenious trick. He stood on the seat and unscrewed a connection so that the pipe, just balanced, would part when the plug was pulled, soaking the next comer. He lurked to watch the success of his ruse but the 'ever flush' poured such torrents of water that he became alarmed. The indignant victim had gone to matron for dry clothes so it was the perpetrator who came to report this astonishing "accident" to the Headmaster's wife. Inevitably there was no one else free to mop up. This boy, Who Shall Be Nameless, was all innocent

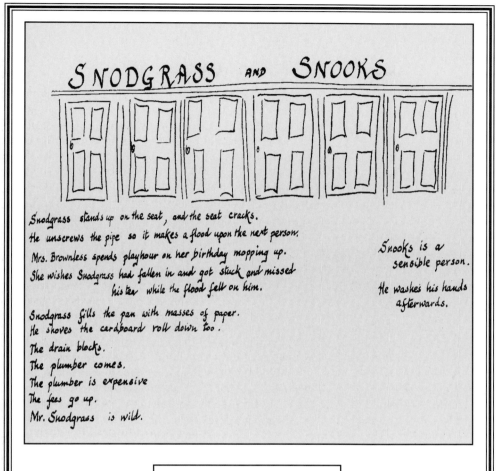

SNODGRASS AND SNOOKS

Snodgrass stands up on the seat, and the seat cracks.
He unscrews the pipe so it makes a flood upon the next person.
Mrs. Brownless spends playhour on her birthday mopping up.
She wishes Snodgrass had fallen in and got stuck and missed
his tea while the flood fell on him.

Snodgrass fills the pan with masses of paper.
He shoves the cardboard roll down too.

The drain blocks.
The plumber comes.
The plumber is expensive
The fees go up.
Mr. Snodgrass is wild.

Snooks is a
sensible person.

He washes his hands
afterwards.

---

surprise and as the HM's wife could not prove her suspicions she could only thank him for reporting it promptly. Little did

> **SNOOKS AND SNODGRASS CARTOONS**
>
> *This was one of a series which appeared on the school notice board in the 1960s.*

In Lambrook's earliest days many of the boys had handles to their names. By 1900 the nobility went to Wixenford, now

he know as he trotted off to bed with the satisfaction of a job well done and having been thanked for it as well, that the headmaster's wife had hoped to spend her birthday evening quite otherwise. At least this experience ensured that all working parts were concealed when the lavatories were rebuilt some years later.

Ludgrove, because, legend says, someone scribbled on the wall "Lord X is wet". Graffiti is nowadays dignified as an art form but not at Lambrook where much paint and headmasterly energy has been expended over years in keeping the loos as they should be.

3

THE REV. F. D. BROWNE
HEADMASTER
1904–1930

THE FIRST TEN YEARS: 1904–1914

THE REVEREND FRANCIS DESHON BROWNE was a tall, calm man with a level gaze and broad shoulders, metaphorically as well as physically. He came as headmaster to Lambrook in 1904 with his wife and daughter. Dr. Thompson, Vicar of Winkfield, later described him as "a rare and exceptional personality, full of kindness and real humility who won the esteem and affection of all – a Christian gentleman."

Looking back after two world wars and several social upheavals it is easy to think the early years of this century must have been a stable and prosperous time at Lambrook. This is far from the truth.

Marjorie Browne was 6 when they arrived at Lambrook "and my most vivid remembrance of the next ten years was seeing Mum and Dad sitting at the end of each term poring over the ledgers, trying to work out how they could pay off all their debts. I felt we might go to prison any day. Mum put her £2000 dowry into buying the school and they borrowed all the rest – a hundred here and a hundred there – from all sorts of people. They only began to see daylight in 1914 when of course the war came and all expenses soared. How on earth they paid for the Chapel I can't imagine. That was built their first year."

Financially things were grim: Mr. Browne had paid for the goodwill of over 50 boys but there were only 35 when he arrived and seven teaching staff had still to be paid. Locally there was ill will as the Brownes – he was 33 – were thought too young to run the place. Domestically it was difficult as most of the 18 servants left with the Mansfields. Coal for open fires had to be taken up to the top floor as well as to the classrooms, and water had to be carried to the dormitories. The hasty departure of Marjorie's governess, rumoured to have got off with one of the gardeners, added fuel to the village gossips' fires. Domestic troubles persisted until the arrival of Blanche as parlour maid in 1910 who stayed for 19 years and of Day, who was not only a fine cook but – after her drunken predecessors – a stabilising influence below stairs.

Mr. Browne was a good athlete, with a Cambridge degree in classics and was ordained during his first year of teaching at Cordwalles, then in St. Pirans' buildings at Maidenhead. When he came to Lambrook seven years later, a colleague came with him from Cordwalles. A.E.Fernie was a superb teacher of English with blues for both cricket and soccer. Moreover he was a wonderfully patient and kindly man.

Later Mr. Fernie spoke of the headmaster's concern about the "atmosphere of fear" and the uneasy truce between staff and boys. Mr.Browne was determined to bridge this gulf. Legend has it that he waited unseen near the wicket of the Stone Pitch (Lambrook's version of playground cricket) and when the batsman was out, he stepped forward and picked up the bat. The fielders were eager, the ball was bowled and the batsman lofted it over the roof saying 'Six and out'. He then joined the fielders almost before the boys realised it was their headmaster playing Stone Pitch with them. Thereafter they were to take the company of masters very much for granted. Mr. Fernie said it was a quiet revolution.

The Gray brothers in the 1890s had said that the senior master I.G.Overton "was a bully, disliked and feared by one and all. He was the one man on the staff who noticeably made favourites." Marjorie Browne remembered his fiery temper and bad table manners – especially with rice pudding. He had a financial share in Lambrook and great was the relief when he left, Mr. Fernie having bought him out.

Mr. Browne had used the Star as his study at first. IGO's sitting room was on the right by the front door and Mr.Browne took this room over when IGO left. The telephone, on the wall by the door, was too high for the young Marjorie to reach: she was intrigued by it but slightly scared too. This room gets all the morning sun and Peter Dalglish, carpeted for some misdemeanour, was so enthralled by a rare butterfly on the terrace outside that he did not hear a word of the headmasterly wrath. The might of the headmasterly wrist (Mr. Browne was a powerful golf and fives player) could not so easily be ignored.

The present study overlooking the tennis court was the Brownes' dining room. Here they pored over the ledgers and here Mrs. Browne, formerly Miss Amy Morres, did her wonderful tapestry. She was one of a family of ten, five brothers and five sisters. One brother who had been a prospector lived for a time in the Lambrook summerhouse, "not liking to be in a house" said Ronald Colles. "We called him The Wild Man. He showed us how to light a fire using sticks opened up with a sharp knife like a fircone". One of Mrs. Browne's sisters, Auntie Betty (Miss Morres), came to teach Marjorie and some junior boys in the Star. She helped in various ways for ten years and was affectionately remembered. Her vivacious letters were a delight, beautifully written even when she was over 90.

The coaching of games took a sharp upturn in the early days of the new regime. Mr. Browne "had a mania for fresh air and exercise" according to his daughter and was a skilful games player. Also Mr.Fernie soon transmitted his enthusiasm to the boys. "The game must be played for its own sake and for the sake of the school, not for individual glory." Before long there was a Star Cricket XI: Cuthbert Norris Elye remembered the needle match against Sunningdale in 1906. Jack Pedley had been at the wicket for ages (he made 124 not out) when the 9th wicket fell and CLNE had to go in to bat. As he set off on the long walk to the wicket, Mr. Browne said "Don't be a poopynobble" and Mr. Fernie said "Now don't come back till you and Pedley have done it!" They did it.

Another cricket match was enlivened by a battle on the pitch: Niger, the Brownes' black spaniel was nearly killed by Togo, the Fernies' bulldog. The boys were enthralled, said Marjorie.

Away matches were exciting events: all too often they were cancelled for foul weather or because one or other school had an infectious illness. The six miles in a horse drawn brake to Wixenford or Sunningdale could mean a lovely long half day away from school.

Once a victorious team returned in great excitement and the sudden burst of cheering as they turned in at the Lambrook gate startled the horses so that the brake crashed against the stone pillar. Ever since then, in coach or minibus today, teams have turned into the drive in silence and not until they pass the two beech trees does the captain say "One, two, three..." Then the cheering starts, with thumbs up for a victory and thumbs horizontal for a draw. A defeated team returns in silence.

Parental visits were rare so Parents' Day in June was eagerly awaited. The Fathers versus Sons Cricket match was an all day affair and several times Mr. Browne engaged a regimental band to play during the afternoon. "How he afforded it, I do not know!" said Marjorie. The ladies wore dresses to the ground and the strawberry tea on the lawn was long remembered

JACK PEDLEY ABOUT 1906
With the Laundry and the old fives court.

by boys who loved the grandeur and excitement of the day. Their memories have played them false though in effacing the ghastly cold wet Saturdays in June that those legendary golden summers produced. *The Chronicle* speaks of "tea indoors after all", of "torrential rainstorms" and "biting winds", of the band having to play in the schoolroom but that "Yip -I- Addy saved everyone from melancholy." In 1911 they had "a fine Parents' Day at last!"

In 1907 Walter Roberts won a scholarship to Winchester, proof that a more benign climate in the school had not spelled ruin to the academic standard, and the school spent a whole day on the river. Lantern slides of this occasion show boys in straw boaters scrambling into a high horse drawn brake with a top hatted driver on the box and a white flannelled, straw boatered master chatting to a smartly hatted lady in an ankle length dress. Never again was an individual success celebrated in such a leisurely fashion. Thereafter the steady stream of scholarships to public schools and awards in the navy examination were celebrated with a half holiday.

The whole school went to the funeral of King Edward VII in Windsor in 1910, hiring every available horse drawn vehicle in Bracknell for the occasion. Everyone enjoyed this outing except S.K. Rutherford who said it was the one horrible memory of

```
LAMBROOK, BRACKNELL
1907.
GENERAL INSTRUCTIONS to the SERVANTS


    Bedroom and Dormitory slop water
must be emptied into a water closet, or
the
slop sink, and not into any other sink.
When slops are poured down a water clos-
et, the hinged seat must first be lifted
up. Should any slop water be spilled
over on
to the safe or woodwork it must be at
once wiped up.
    The water closet and slop sink
basins and traps must be kept perfectly
clean, a hard fibre brush being used to
remove any stains from the basins, and
the underside of the seats are to be
wiped dry.
    If any leakage or defect is observed
in any of the pipes, taps, or valves,
attention should at once be called to
it.
```

This notice hung beside the slop sink on the top floor of Lambrook. There were few W.C.s among the dormitories where 50 boys slept and the school lavatories seemed miles away so each boy had a chamber pot under his bed. These were emptied at the slop sink each morning by the dormitory maids.

his otherwise happy years at Lambrook. He, being new and young, had to travel in a victoria with Mrs.Holloway, the matron. He thought Holloway prison had been named after her.

These ten years before World War One saw Lambrook evolving into the clearly recognisable ancestor of today's school. *The Lambrook Chronicle* began in 1909. It is still an annual production in a dark green cover containing, as Mr.Browne's first Editorial put it, "a humble account of the life we lead, the honours we reap, the games we play." Readers were warned not to expect "much novelty or any great literary merit" though the boys' contributions over the years have produced plenty of both.

The school colours were changed from the black and red of Mr.Mansfield's time to dark green. Boys wore dark green caps and blazers for cricket with white flannel trousers. Senior boys wore straw boaters. The old Norfolk suits were gradually ousted by a grey flannel suit with high revers, sometimes with a waistcoat, and long trousers. The photographs show a variety of suits and materials. Some boys wore dark grey flannel trousers with a black Eton jacket on Sundays and the hated starched Eton collar.

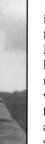

A.E.FERNIE
taught at Lambrook between 1904 and 1921. His were the history lessons which inspired Walter Sellar to write "1066 And All That."

When the lake was drained for cleaning in 1911 it was never refilled because it was felt to be unhealthily close to the house. Marjorie, a rather solitary child, felt its loss keenly. The school carpenter, Mr.Berry, had made her a flat bottomed punt and the island with the pine tree became her favourite place for reading. Senior boys had the Sunday afternoon privilege of using this punt and should have known better than to maroon the young Marjorie there one day. Very old Old Boys have spoken of drifting off to sleep in the top floor dormitories listening to the sounds of masters skating by moonlight on this little lake.

Dorothy Williams – of whom more later as she became a staunch friend of Lambrook – was the youngest of six children who lived in a labourer's cottage in Winkfield Row. Her hopscotch drawn in the dust at the side of the road lasted several weeks as horse drawn carts drove down the middle and cars, which blew more dust about, were rare. Local children were strict in their observance of the right seasons for their games: preparations could be made, whistles carved, conkers collected, whips cut from the hedges for tops, but until the right day came, Candlemas or Little St.Martin or whatever, the actual game might not start. Then all was feverish activity with contests until the craze had worn off and it was time to prepare for the next, perhaps hoops or skipping. These seasons lasted about six weeks.

Similar activities are mentioned often by pre World War 1 Lambrook boys. Yo-yos, chess, balsa wood carving, story writing, conkers or marbles used to hit the school almost like a plague, lasting for some weeks. The seasons for these crazes were not as sharply defined as the local children's, perhaps because Lambrook boys led such timetabled lives and their spare time was at a premium.

Visits from parents were rare partly because travelling was slow, and partly to minimise the chance of infection coming into the community: an epidemic disrupted work and games for weeks. Nevertheless there was plenty going on, concerts – sometimes two a term – with boys and staff, lectures on subjects as varied as *The humour of Punch* and *The Balkan tangle* and visiting preachers on Sundays. In 1914 B.W.Tucker gave a lecture on reptiles. This was reported as a very good lecture and the first one given by a boy in the school. Photographs of school plays show some grand costumes: the *Babes in the Wood* was specially written and Archie Forbes was an elderly governess. He wore a huge hat and looked like his own grandmother. S.K. Rutherford was Second Robin and spoke feelingly sixty years later of the difficulty of learning to hop with a pillow fore and aft.

Three boys who arrived within a few months of each other, expecting to stay only a few years at Lambrook, spent most of their lives there. Guy Cameron was a new boy in 1906. He later returned to teach and became headmaster. Ted Coxhead came in 1906, as gardener's boy. He became Head Gardener in 1921 and his knowledge and care of the grounds and buildings was immense. Archie Forbes was a new boy in 1907 and he too returned later to teach and became headmaster. These three, about whom more later, served Lambrook for 110 years in all, and died within a few weeks of each other in 1956.

The kindly Sergeant Major Butt was still going strong. He left in 1916 after 25 years as "the kingpin of the place". He arranged transport to matches and to the station: he bought the boys' tickets and saw to their luggage. He looked after the stationery and when he handed out yet another wooden handled pen with a steel nib, and wanted the youngster to take care of it, would say "All the way from Timbuctoo".

He had taught over 400 boys to swim taking "endless trouble with timid boys who were frightened to launch out into the deep." Confidence in him enabled them to perform gymnastic feats usually considered beyond the abilities of young boys. Ronald Colles recalled Sergeant Butt "feigning anger with a belt in his hand, chasing a disruptive pupil round the gym and carefully hitting all the equipment but never the boy." Archie Forbes was very bad at gym – he was far too lanky having reached 6 foot when he was 12 – but he remembered Sergeant Butt with affection, even the stern reproof "FORBES, go laast for laaffing". Sergeant Butt was held in high regard by the village boys. There was a rifle range in the gravel pit at the top of Chavey Down and there he taught them to shoot, Dorothy Williams' brothers among them. He became the tenant of a country pub near Henley and died there aged nearly 90. Audley Gray said he was "one of the finest men I have ever met."

By 1913 the school had expanded from 35 boys to 59 and new changing rooms were needed. The old carpentry shop under the clock was made into changing rooms and "the Bibble" at the end of the classroom passage was used variously as a dark room, a dump and the barber's den. Here came a stream of boys to have their hair cut at record speed while the hair on the floor piled up so that the barber was almost knee deep by lunchtime. Rumour had it that he wore a wig and that leaving boys might be shown it if they swore a mighty oath of secrecy.

THE FIRST WORLD WAR
1914–1918.

The two immediate effects of World War 1 at Lambrook were knitting and drill. "Mrs. Browne and Miss Morres have been busy for many weeks with the knitters. It is hoped that quite a number of scarves and mittens will find their way to the soldiers and sailors at Christmas time." Thirteen boys were commended because "they finished what they undertook." What tangles of wool and dropped stitches those words conjure up.

Ronald Colles was 10: "Many boys made wooden swords in the carpenter's shop. We also attempted a form of drill in which we started in single line, numbered and formed 'two deep'. Without further numbering we got the order 'Form fours' which resulted in chaos. Button hole badges with the flags of the allies were much worn and new badges with more flags were required each term as more nations became involved. D.F.O.Dangar (then aged 11) was a leading authority on the progress of hostilities."

When Mr. Browne wrote the editorial for the 1914 *Chronicle*, the "War to end all wars" was 3 months old and he tried as far as possible to avoid the subject. Two members of staff, due to come in September, had enlisted instead: Kenneth Dodgson, a fine young master, who had just gone to Salisbury Theological College, joined the army and was killed 6 months later. An Old Boy, 2nd.Lieut.Auriol Round, aged 22, died from wounds in the first month and there was well justified anxiety about numerous others.

The obituaries during the next four years make sombre reading. The figures are stark – 25 Old Boys killed – but the reality was worse both in terms of the country's loss and in personal grief – two brothers and even three died in some families. Apart from their successes at school and university, these youngsters, mostly under 25, made deep impressions on their friends as letters of condolence show. "His life, though short, must have been a help to many". "He was always keeping people cheerful". "He was just such a one as we can least afford to lose". "Cheerful and merry under the most miserable of conditions, he was always busy and volunteering for every work that was to be done." "We look back with gratitude for his kindly influence."

The youngest Old Boy to die was Bombardier A.V.Preston. Described as "a large person" when he left Lambrook in 1912, he was "one of the kindest hearted boys in the school." He enlisted under age and was about to be commissioned when he was killed in France aged 16.

Almost the oldest was Lieut. Raymond Asquith aged 36, son of the late Prime Minister. A scholar of Balliol and President of the Union, he won several university prizes on his way to a 1st class degree and was elected a Fellow of All Souls. He was considered the most brilliant man of his year and "one whom the country can ill afford to lose."

Two of the obituaries reflect the national fervour : "Basil Davis was never very strong," wrote Mr. Browne, and he spent some of his school-days in a wheelchair. "So anxious was he to do his part for his country that he underwent an operation" and at length got his wings in the Royal Flying Corps. He was killed within a month of getting out to France. His C.O. wrote "Your son was a keen and reliable pilot with any amount of dash. In another trip the same day he had flown over to an enemy aero-drome and fired about 200 rounds into the hangars there."

The war indirectly caused Cyril Dangar's death. "He was rejected for the army in 1917 on account of heart trouble. Determined to serve in some capacity he joined the English section of the French Red Cross, and drove an ambulance until after the Armistice. His was a very strenuous life during these years, his section being twice awarded the Croix de Guerre for bravery and devotion to duty." He went up to Cambridge in the summer term but was not well and died in October 1919 aged 20.

In the community where these young men had so recently been lively schoolboys, their deaths were felt as personal losses. Keeping the school running smoothly with staff shortages was an additional strain.

Small wonder that Marjorie Browne, now 18, who left her school in the west country in 1916 hoping to go to France as an ambulance driver, found her parents "grey with worry" on her return to Lambrook and felt she must join them as general factotum. She did secretarial work for her father in the mornings after she had mown the lawns and tennis court at 6 a.m. with a push mower, and done masses of washing up and bedmaking. Bill Weston was the chauffeur and he also looked after the electricity generator in the back yard. When he was called up, Marjorie took on this job as well, filling the battery cells with distilled water and turning a huge wheel to start the engine. Her worst job though was working the magic lantern for lectures. It was a carbon arc lamp and the gap between the two carbons had to be judged to a nicety : if they were too close, everything got covered with sooty black bits. "That magic lantern was the bane of my life" said Marjorie 60 years later.

Cricket, football and rugger were sometimes curtailed by weather or illness but gym, swimming, Rugby fives, golf and rifle shooting were all taught. The gym competitions were elaborate and the expert judges from Aldershot regularly paid tribute to the teaching of Mr. C. E. Hartley. They would have thought still more of him if they had known that he taught senior French and junior maths, and took endless pains over the golfers, several of whom blossomed later into Blues.

Christopher Hanbury's abiding memory was of the cold. His Letts Schoolboy Diary for 1916 reveals this and the busy monotony of everyday life.

January 30: Mr. Fernie starts a book called Beltain the smith.

February 15: Mr.Browne takes us for a walk in the afternoon and he lets us rag in the woods. I get a quarter star for Latin.

February 24: Stop in schoolroom in morning because of snow. I get an impot from Bug. Most boys have a snowball fight but I go for a walk because of chilblains.

February 25: I do not go to gym because of chilblains. We all go to the woods and have a snowfight. I make ammunition.

February 26: 10 inches of snow. Most change and have a snowfight. I go out a little and knock snow off shrubs. Flick paper with elastic most of the afternoon.

Sunday February 27: Go for a long walk in the afternoon. We have to put our stockings over our Eton trousers. It is very sloshy.

March 1: In prep Turner and I very nearly get a stripe for talking. We just do ordinary talking in the dorm.

March 2: We do the boar War (sic!) for prep which is very interesting indeed.I am put in silence by Turner for making a noise in the dorm.

March 4: One game of rugger, most play golf and I walk about in the afternoon. Very good conjuror instead of lecture. I go on with my story.

March 6: It's my birthday so in the morning I got a parcel of games and books and two letters. Don't go to gym because of chilblains. Mr. Browne gives us all vocab. 49 to write out. Go for walk in morning. In afternoon all play rugger. I walk about with Turner. Get oranges for fruit.Come in early and finish impot. Get my chilblains bound up before tea. Bulleid put in silence by Matron in the evening."

March 7: Shrove Tuesday: Stop in schoolroom in morning because of snow. For lunch we have pancakes but there aren't enough for second helps.

March 9: Do ordinary things but I get mumps in the morning with others so of course we aren't allowed out but just stop in the library and rag about all morning.

March 10: We are in the dorm all day, we have bread and butter and tea for breakfast. We have our necks bound up. Have soup and rice for dinner. In the afternoon, read then we are put to sleep. Have tea, read wash and have beds made, then biscuits and milk, read Bible, say prayers and go to sleep.

Sunday 12 March: Wake up in the morning with my mumps on both sides. Read one of Peal's papers as my book is finished. Then Mr. Browne comes into the dorm, says prayers and reads the second lesson. Play and read till lunch, soup and custard. Go to sleep then rag about. Miss Morres comes and gives us oranges. Rag about and then have tea.

March 14: Have quite a good night. Mr.Browne comes up and gives our Latin sentences back of which we have to do the corrections. Cottage pie and chocolate mould for lunch then read and go to sleep and rag about till tea. I rag about till light is put out and then go to sleep.

March 15: In the night, Bulleid has a nightmare so we have a nightlight so Boby and I have a long talk."

Friday 24 March: In the morning we do ordinary things and go for a walk in break but in French Vlasto lets off a stink bomb and it makes an awful smell so he is reported to FDB. In the evening we sing *The Story of the Cross.*

The entries dwindled as the weather improved: the last one is succinct: "Do nothing."

Two innovations in 1917 were Boy Scouts and the new pronunciation of Latin. Mr Browne clearly viewed both with misgivings. However, the Scouts were an instant success. General Baden Powell was a friend of Mr. A.D.Power and often stayed at Brockdale next to Orchard House. The Lambrook Scouts were regularly inspected by the Great Man himself. Soon there were 35 boys in 7 patrols and each patrol had a garden. Naturalist, Swimmer, Musician, Pioneer and Handyman were the first badges awarded and one patrol built an Indian teepee. "This was quite a success and is now to be seen generally with Wardrop crouching inside it." (He was later the manager of Heathrow when it was becoming an international airport. Perhaps he really liked crouching inside half built constructions.)

Wolf Cubs began in 1918 and soon Mrs. Fernie and Miss Morres had them growing vegetables too. "We were very nervous about food rationing" wrote Mr. Browne, "and all thought we were going to dwindle away to mere skeletons." Christopher Hanbury thought the food was very good: "even with wartime rationing there never seemed to be any shortage." Nevertheless, fears about food rationing and real difficulties over rail travel caused Parents' Day to be cancelled in 1918. We were "very thankful that

we managed to avoid the all prevailing epidemic of influenza". Spanish flu caused deaths all over the country that cold winter. Lucky Lambrook boys had 3 weeks' skating at Warfield Park.

Meanwhile solid progress was made in work according to the headmaster. "The foundation of success in the summer is laid by the quiet 'grind' of the Winter and Easter terms. In a Spartan like way we have got up for early school: it is rather a struggle, that first leap out of bed, but if the cocoa is hot and the classroom fires blazing there is some compensation and there is no doubt that a lot of good work is done before breakfast."

Boys were now going to more than 16 public schools, as well as Osborne for the navy, and were usually placed in high forms thanks to their good grounding. The steady trickle of scholarships rose to 6 in 1921 and Mr Browne wrote the words which have echoed at Lambrook ever since: "We do not cram our candidates – intending scholars do no more work than anyone else in the upper school." He sounded another note whose timelessness is almost comic – it could have been penned by any of Lambrook's headmasters at any time in either century: "Getting into the public schools is not the easy matter it was a few years ago and no one can afford to waste any time in any class."

Parents were beating a path to the door because of Lambrook's reputation for sound teaching and all round care. In 1914 the school was considered full with 58 boys. There were 78 boys four years later and 86 soon after, at which figure it remained for some years. More room had to be found.

Boys first went out to sleep at Orchard House in 1914, seven of them (considered highly privileged) in the care of Mr. and Mrs.Fernie. The dining hall was a tight spot so six boys in turn joined Mr. and Mrs. Browne in her dining room, now the study. IC, a new bottom form, was started. At first they worked in the Star with Miss Morres but soon expanded into the big schoolroom which accommodated two classes and two masters for the next thirty years – an unpopular arrangement.

A new form, Remove, was started in 1918 with the formidable Miss Gull as form mistress, preparing seven candidates ("by no means strong ones") for Common Entrance. She was a gifted teacher, taking Greek in Remove, French and Latin throughout the school and the 3 Rs with juniors, "all with keenness and skill" said Mr Browne. She also ran the Wolf Cubs. As they marched past the saluting base one day and the Sixer said "Eyes right" a bad boy put out his tongue at Miss Gull. At the ensuing court martial Mr Browne, as president, was hard put to preserve due decorum.

At the end of 1918 he looked back with relief and forward with hope: "We have much to be grateful for. The school is full of what Mr. Ian Hay, the novelist, calls 'The Right Stuff'. Many who would have done us the honour of sending their sons to Lambrook have been unable to do so owing to lack of room and no further entries can be made until 1920. Now that we are full we must see to it that the school keeps up the reputation won."

NEW BLOOD: 1919–1930
with junior partners
A.H.FORBES from 1922 and G.F.CAMERON from 1925

The arrival of new young masters was heartening especially since two of them were Old Boys. Guy Cameron was at Lambrook from 1906 to 1909 and won a scholarship to Uppingham where he also had a distinguished career. From there he went to Oxford in 1913, to read classics and played cricket, rugger and hockey for Brasenose College. When World War 1 started he joined the Queen's Own Cameron Highlanders and was badly wounded in France in 1915. For forty years this unhealed wound in his side gave him trouble. Few of his colleagues realised this.

Having spent four years in and out of hospital Guy was appointed by the Rev.F.D.Browne to teach senior classics and coach cricket at Lambrook in 1919. He was a fine games coach and an able teacher. Two years later he and Marjorie Browne were married – the first wedding in the

1926

On the left behind the seated ladies stand Phil Squarey and Mr Parkinson.
Seated fouth from left, Miss Gull, Mr Reginald Clough, Mrs Amy Browne wth grandaughter Anne at her feet, The Rev.F.D.Browne, Archie & Flora Forbes, Gerald Chamberlain, Marjorie & Guy Cameron with Jean, Mr. G.F.E.Abbott. The top row of boys between the two trees are, from the left, J.C.Hope, Harington, J.O.J.Stevens, Owen Prichard, Becher. Hamilton, Ronald Lunt. Looking over Archie Forbes' shoulder is, W.G.Nicholson, between C.G.B.McClure (behind F.D.B.) and M.M.J.Stevens (between Archie & Flora).
Many more were identified by J.O.J.Stevens nearly sixty years later.

43

Lambrook Chapel. They lived at Orchard House during those early years and had two daughters. In 1925 he became a junior partner.

While he was a boy at Lambrook, between 1907 and 1912, Archie Forbes had resolved to work there one day. He was 3 years younger than Guy and followed him to Uppingham and then to France with the Queens' Royal Regiment. He was wounded and awarded the M.C. ("for saving the Colonel's toast from burning", he said). Joining up had curtailed his Uppingham time but his time in the trenches left him with insomnia so bad that he hardly slept when he got to Oriel College, Oxford and only lasted a year. He was an able games player and a gifted pianist. On joining the Lambrook staff in 1920, he learned the names and faces in the school groups of the eight years he had been away, and thereafter it was a source of shame if he failed to recognise anyone.

In 1921, Archie became a junior partner with Mr. Browne and in 1924, he married Flora Keyes. Walter Sellar, his old friend from schooldays and shortly to write *1066 and All That,* was Archie's best man. Archie bought an acre of land from the school and built Brook Cottage. They had two daughters, Isla and Rona, naming them off the map of Scotland. (Fortunately there were no more children of this marriage – they were destined to be called Muck, Eigg and Rum.)

BROOK COTTAGE

Archie Forbes bought an acre of land from the Rev. F.D. Browne and had Brook Cottage built in 1924 when he and Flora were married. The bungalow was solidly built but the money did not stretch to electric light. They used paraffin lamps. At first they could not afford a drive and guests were escorted along a path of planks by Archie with a torch and umbrella.

Lambrook used Brook Cottage to house staff and sometimes boys for almost fifty years.

ARCHIE FORBES' CAR, AN AUTOCRAT

In 1924 there were only two cars in Winkfield Row.

Extra chores and unexpected duties came the way of Guy and Archie, the youngest members of staff. They used to "volunteer" alternately, kicking each other under the table when Mr. Browne asked if "someone" would please undertake this or that.

Cars were still few. Mr. Browne had a 2 seater Rover "with no windscreen and not much of a hood" said Marjorie. Archie's was a 2 seater Autocrat with an aluminium bonnet: they were the first two cars in Winkfield Row. Mr. Bailey had a bicycle repair shop at Maiden's Green and employed a saddler, Mr. Murrell, who was kept busy repairing saddlery and harness for horses working on farms, in delivery carts, in gigs and dogcarts. When Archie asked Mr. Bailey if he would consider mending punctures in car tyres as well as bicycle tyres, Mr. Bailey shook his head and thought the car craze would soon pass. However, he had second thoughts and his business prospered. His name is now truly on the map as Bailey's Garage gave the name to Bailey's cross roads.

The departure of Mr. and Mrs. Fernie in 1921 to open Melbreck, a pre preparatory school, was a great loss. He had been a kindly influence and a wonderful teacher in class and on the games field for 17 years. He enjoyed the boys' company and they his. "A marvellous fund of story and anecdote enabled him to invest the dry bones of history and geography with romance and interest." Posterity owes him a great debt – he inspired *1066 and all that*. Walter Sellar and Archie Forbes had sat together in every class at Lambrook, enjoying Mr. Fernie's memorable history lessons – "King John was a BAD THING". When *1066 and all that* was published in 1929, Mr. Fernie recognised its source and wrote delightedly to Archie Forbes asking "What has Sellar done now?"

The names of the masters whom Mr. Browne appointed during these ten years awake lively memories. He may have found the boys a good deal easier to cope with than the staff. Two young masters in 1921, Reggie Clough, (statuesque), and Tony Crawshaw (neat and nimble) were a great double act. They loved disguises and led the scouts some energetic paper chases. One day Reggie, wearing a general's uniform and riding Queenie, the mower pony, inspected the scouts. He fell off on arrival and Tony, as his adjutant, leaned a long ladder against the patient pony and helped the general climb slowly back on to his charger. Another day the scouts with Archie were firelighting in the field by Brockhill Farm when two painted savages beating dinner gongs and wearing only underpants came gallivanting up the road yelling horribly. Rounding them up ended the afternoon excitingly in the days when nobody went out on the King's highway half dressed.

One Ascot week they turned some signposts round. Reggie in policeman's uniform, then stood at a crossroads directing cars in chaotic circles until Tony, his snout in a cloth cap, tipped him the wink that a proper bobby was on the way.

When Tony Crawshaw came in to the common room one break and announced that he and Miss Warner (the comely junior mistress) had just got engaged, Reggie assumed it was a wild jape and, referring to the other lady member of staff (elderly and not beautiful), exclaimed "Where's Miss Gull?" and dashed off in mock pursuit. When he realised that the Crawshaw-Warner engagement was for real he had to do a quick about face.

The Crawshaws left in 1924 to run a pre-preparatory school. Reggie Clough left in 1928, was ordained next year and married soon after. Both couples sent sons to Lambrook and both families returned briefly to the staff during World War Two. Reggie's son, also RMcKC but known as Dick, taught at Lambrook for 7 years in the 1950s. He was a fine artist.

C.R.B. Wrenford, who won prizes through his schooldays at Lambrook, Uppingham and Oxford, had a fantastic memory. Old Boys treated him rather as a mobile reference book. Asked about the weather on Parents' Day twenty years earlier he sat silent and, when the talk had long since passed to other topics, he spoke as from a great height: "Actually the day dawned clear and bright but rain began to fall about 11 and lasted till lunchtime so the match started late." Sceptics checked and found him right. In the 1920s he taught briefly at Lambrook where his infallibility proved tiresome so two colleagues planned a small revenge. Another, bicycling back to Brockhill, heard cries and saw a group at the brick bridge over the Lamb. Two masters were holding CRBW over the parapet by the ankles ready to dip his head in and out of the water. The cries were his "confession" audible right back in Winkfield Row "Yes, yes, I am a fool, I am a fool."

Gerald Chamberlain came to Lambrook in 1924 and stayed until his early death in 1946. He was a gentle giant who had captained his college boat at Cambridge. He taught Geography, was a wonderful naturalist and made several films of life at Lambrook in the 1930s. "Those who dug in the gardens, or went birds' nesting, or delighted in contrivances mechanical and electrical – all consulted "Jumbo". He was an unselfish friend." wrote an Old Boy.

He did the electrics for the plays in the 1930s written by Guy Roberts with music by Archie Forbes. One about the Spartans at Thermopylae involved an explosion and the flash contrived by Jumbo with magnesium was cataclysmic. Flakes of magnesium floated to the ceiling of the schoolroom and wafted up the stone stairs. Warm air then took them up and up and up to the dormitories. Next morning every room was covered with big grey flakes. As soon as any door was opened the flakes floated to the ceilings again and it was weeks before all four storeys were finally cleared.

Phil Squarey, another Old Boy, arrived in 1926 having spent his Cambridge time "working hard at rugger, cricket and hockey and playing with the history tripos." He had a quick wit, a first class eye for ball games and was at his best playing something unorthodox like ice hockey on bumpy ice. He was a voluble and energetic coach whose stentorian rebuke to a lazy player was "BACK TO YOUR KENNEL, BOY!"

The Squarey husband and wife team used to challenge the Forbes husband and wife team at every imaginable sport, fives, tennis, golf, tiddly winks, etc and the honours were fairly even. The Squareys were the more dashing players but the Forbes pair employed low cunning. Placing their return shots between the two Squareys (where either could have returned it if the other had allowed) caused such furious poaching and arguments that both usually missed it. Deuce again.

Jock Hunt arrived in 1927, in plus fours like Phil Squarey, to teach French and handicrafts. When he left eight years later it was with the headmaster's secretary as his wife, to run their own school, Beech Hall, Macclesfield. It has flourished under two generations of Hunts.

When Pat Cowley, Hugh Hope, Ronald Lunt and John Stevens, all boys of this era, met fifty years later to reminisce. RL said Guy Cameron was a super teacher; PC thought Miss Gull very good; HH remembered being kept in to learn lines; JOJS remembered learning the collect each Sunday; RL and JOJS both had to have Yardil, a garlic based medicine, in milk; RL had whooping cough in the epidemic of 1922 and "Mrs.Browne read to the survivors"; PC said there was no fun after lights out; RL thought they were "very reasonably treated over fresh air and exercise"; HH remembered the walks and Archie "signalling a change of direction with his semaphore arm"; PC hated the walks: he sat in a puddle one day saying "Down with England, up with Ireland"; HH remembered Mr. Browne's maroon coloured car which JOJS thought was a Windsor; PC said away matches were a great pleasure; JOJS remembered the music master losing his temper at a choir practice and kicking the piano; they all remembered the sweets, with Archie opening "shop" after lunch, 5 bullseyes for a penny, said HH and they had twopence to spend; JOJS said there was always the chance of an explosion to liven up a lantern slide lecture; PC played chess all the way up the school; HH enjoyed story writing on Saturday evenings and reading the *Illustrated London News*; RL remembered Funnel, the little bootman who could walk upright into the casing of the school clock to wind it; JOJS was captain of the Dragon dormitory when Bobby Walpole swallowed his tiepin which occasioned some excitement. He was given cotton wool and banana sandwiches to eat – he had a title to inherit.

By 1930 the strong family feeling extended to Old Boys' gatherings and cricket weeks. At the Old Boys' Dinner in 1924 the guest of honour was Colonel S, then a very old man. During the dinner "he turned yellow and then pea green" but was revived by Cuthbert Norris Elye and Guy Cameron "with fresh air and port" in time to make his speech – here given in full: "When I was at Lambrook we weren't pampered – beer for breakfast and it was all prepared in the dungeons which had green moss on the floor."

Lambrook under the Rev.F.D.Browne was paternalistic in the best sense. Every member of the community mattered and knew that the Brownes minded about each one. Among many tributes was the recollection of an anxious mother reassured by her son's first letter home which simply said "Mr. Browne is 'alright'." His successors were already known to all, so after 26 years at the helm, he left Lambrook to become vicar of Waltham St.Lawrence. He was 60.

LEATHER OVERSHOES
were worn by Queenie, the pony, who pulled the heavy mower on the cricket field during the 1920's.

A DIGRESSION ON THE CHAPEL

THE BUILDING OF THE CHAPEL WAS A VENTURE OF FAITH. Though money was scarce, the Rev.F.D.Browne put the work in hand as soon as he arrived and five months later the Chapel was dedicated by the Bishop of Oxford in February 1905. Mr. Browne wanted the Chapel to be central in the life of the community, connected by a passage to the big schoolroom so that boys could go to daily prayers without having to put on outdoor shoes.

Weekday prayers, Sunday services, confirmation services, memorial services, weddings and baptisms have taken place in the Chapel. The names of the babies are engraved on the silver rose bowl which Old Boys gave Mr.Browne and which now serves as the font. In 1912, thirty Territorials, at camp in Winkfield Row, came one Sunday evening "and the singing was grand". Early Chapel collections included £4.12.6 (double the usual amount) sent to the fund following the loss of the Titanic in 1912. The fare for a Barnardo boy to go out to Canada was £10 and Lambrook sent the money for three boys' fares between 1910 and 1914. One of these boys, John Boggis, wrote back to say he was settling down.

Before the Chapel was built, Lambrook boys walked to Winkfield Church, across the fields in summer. "Mr. and Mrs.Mansfield always conducted the procession to church, he looking very distinguished in the sort of rig one would see at Ascot today."

The first pews were of dark green pine, gradually replaced by the present oak pews, given by leaving boys. In 1929 an oak pew cost £12. The oak panelling round the walls was almost complete by 1939 but a large section, carved and ready in London, was bombed in the blitz and could not be replaced till after the war.

The choir was first robed in 1914, in purple cassocks and white surplices with white collar ruffs. Their number increased to 24 in 1952 when the oak benches in front of the choir stalls were made by Mr.MacDonald, the school handyman. He was delighted to do this: after years of mending desks and lockers, the opportunity to make something fine from good wood was a treat.

Originally E.D.Mansfield had installed an organ in the schoolroom in 1888 and this was moved into the newly built Chapel. Twenty years later it was feeling its age and one service was enlivened by a pipe clattering down on the organist's head. In 1927 the present organ was built and Dr.Charles MacPherson of St.Paul's played at its dedication service.

In 1952 when the organ was overhauled, an electric blower was installed, to the regret of those who had held the privileged position of Organ Blower. Two senior boys whose voices were breaking had the task of pumping air for the organ. In the tiny blowhole, spells of hard work in shirtsleeves alternated with drowsy periods. They could not afford to snooze lest the versicles and responses caught them unawares and "Onward,Christian soldiers" always required a mammoth effort. Archie, who had in his time been chorister, organist and headmaster wrote "Many who held this coveted position will sympathise with the blowers who now find themselves reduced to mere ushers at the back of the Chapel with no water bottles to sustain them on a hot Sunday evening."

Old Boys and friends contributed to the enlargement of the Chapel with the gallery in memory of the two headmaster Old Boys, Guy Cameron and Archie Forbes. It was completed in 1959. The tall stained glass window from the former west wall, in memory of Old Boys who died in World War 1, was placed in the staircase tower. Although the Chapel almost doubled, it cannot accommodate all the parents who like to come to services. The school Carol Service has taken place in Winkfield Church and services have sometimes been relayed to the assembly hall as an overflow.

In the 50s and 60s, before the Exeat started, the service on the Sunday after Parents' Day was attended by over 400 people so the marquee was transformed overnight into a cathedral. It looked and smelled wonderful with huge pots of flowers flanking an oak table with the Chapel cross and candlesticks. It sounded grand too though Mr.Duckett had to manage with a classroom piano wedged more or less upright on the grass. He was a super organist whose war service was spent playing the organ in Cairo Cathedral, the best ever example of wartime redeployment.

Two weddings of headmasters' daughters have been celebrated in Chapel. Marjorie Browne married Guy Cameron, Old Boy and master, in July 1921. The choir stayed on for two festive days after the end of term and sang gloriously on this occasion. One guest said it was "the prettiest wedding I have ever seen."

The wedding in July 1948 of Isla Forbes and the Rev.Philip Brownless, then a parish priest in Southend, was in term time and the boys all came to the reception. The health of the couple was proposed by Guy Cameron.

An entirely Lambrook wedding took place in the Chapel in 1993 when Nicky McGeorge (matron) and Christian Edrich (groundsman) were married by the Rev.John Male (accountant).

The headmasters have taken services and preached regularly in Chapel and have all, including the two ordained headmasters, invited many visiting preachers. Some have become friends of the school like the Rev.John Eddison. An expert in the art of making the Christian faith accessible and attractive, he also holds the longevity record, having preached regularly since his first visit on behalf of the Scripture Union in 1946. Father F, whom Cuthbert Norris Elye said was a "dear old man", achieved a very different record in 1905: repeating the word FRUIT for greater emphasis, his teeth fell out and clattered across the floor.

Resplendent in red cassock was the Dean of Windsor in the 1950s. His grandson of eight was in the school and very nervous about grandfather coming to preach. After the service, grandfather asked grandson if it had been all right and was told "Yes, it was all right this time but promise me you'll never do it again !"

The organ and the choir provide most of the music but the wind band and other instruments lead the singing at family services. Boys contribute also by reading lessons and prayers. The Chapel has been a training ground for future choir members, sidesmen and church wardens. One polite boy taking the collection slightly overdid things by leaning along the row of visitors and saying "Thank you very much" as each coin dropped into the bag. Much care is taken to make Sunday worship stimulating and reflective, uplifting and relevant and the music plays a big part in this.

A steady trickle of Old Boys has been ordained. Some were successful in other spheres before going into the ministry; some have become widely known; others have worked all their days as parish priests. No one this side of the pearly gates can know which aspects of life at Lambrook have contributed to the making of these servants of God and mankind. Certainly the Chapel has played a part.

This summary cannot begin to express the value of the Chapel as the quiet centre of the community. Life, even for eight year olds, becomes ever fuller and it is easy to be swept along on a tide of bustle and noise and peer pressure. Perhaps 'twas ever thus but the Chapel presents an opportunity for a pause, a space for reflection before God, on what the bustle is about and our place in it. Goodness knows how many people have reluctantly gone into Chapel simply because it was on the timetable as the next activity and have there found a different dimension, a refreshing space which has strengthened them for next day, next week, next year.

PHOTOGRAPH BY COURTESY OF JOHN KEELING 1991

THE LAMBROOK CHAPEL

Built in 1904, it was extended in 1958 to accommodate the whole school as well as parents and friends for Sunday services.

4

G. F. CAMERON
HEADMASTER
1930–1939
IN PARTNERSHIP WITH A.H.FORBES

THE RETIREMENT OF THE REV.F.D.BROWNE precipitated several changes. Archie Forbes had been a junior partner for nine years and Guy Cameron for five years but Mr.Browne's financial arrangements for his daughter meant that Guy succeeded to the two thirds share of the senior partner. The Forbes family moved into Orchard House with pleasure but the Camerons were sad to leave it and move into Lambrook whose difficulties Marjorie knew all too well. Guy was not robust and their younger daughter, Jean, was unwell with what was later known as leukaemia. Sadly she was to die only two years later.

What was Guy like? Owen Hickey, at Lambrook in the '30s, remembered him "in flannels at the nets, patiently coaxing the batsman to put his leg across the wicket; reading aloud on Sunday evenings while we sprawled on his study floor, counting and recounting a vanishing hoard of sweets; standing calm above the hubbub of the last day of term, regarding with amused detachment the universal whoops of excitement at the prospect of being quit of his establishment for eight weeks or so. Guy held the affection and respect of many different kinds of people."

The builders moved in first: a vertical slice of four storeys was added to the south side of Lambrook. The boys' bathroom and washroom was enlarged and so was the dininghall by the addition of the study, which now moved to the back of the house. Here the verandah, like the bridge of a ship, overlooked the path where minor miscreants walked in silence instead of cavorting with their fellows in break. There was also a view of the schoolroom. A headmaster with binoculars could see enough to maintain a reputation for omniscience.

Lambrook needed furniture when the Brownes moved out so Mrs. Cameron and Mrs. Forbes went shopping. They flopped on to a large settee in Harrods to compare their lists and budgets. That settee put new life into them and on finding it labelled "Secondhand: £12" they put a triumphant tick on the list. It was in the drawing room for the next sixty years and often gave a comfortable night to an unexpected guest, especially some young Old Boy during the war. Ted Coxhead, coming in early to water the superb houseplants which he had nurtured in the greenhouse, was sometimes tempted to sprinkle a sleeper on the settee.

Orchard House too was altered: two rooms were knocked into one big sitting room, two attics were made into a dormitory and another into the boys' bathroom. Before this there were wash-stands in the dormitories and hot water had been carried up from the kitchen. It was clear by 1930 that the days of cheap labour for such chores had ended. The china washstand bowls ended their days holding fruit salad for the school.

GUY CAMERON

By today's standards, the domestic staff worked long hours and were lowly paid. However service was not then a dirty word and these maids were kindly looked after and were better housed and fed, they said, than they had ever been. Newspaper advertisements, placed where unemployment was high, produced girls glad of residential jobs in order to send money home. Mining areas of Wales were depressed and Lambrook had bevies of Welsh girls who chirruped like bugerigars as they sped about in their green dresses. They did masses of housework: they made the boys' beds, complete with counterpanes: they waited at table, known as "Maidy" by the boys, and washed up: after lunch they changed into black dresses with little white aprons and a gaggle of them with baskets of mending would sit under a tree with Miss Bennett, matron /housekeeper. Sometimes she read to them. After tea they sped round the dormitories again, folding up the counterpanes. Too often a girl in domestic service was lonely: at Lambrook a dozen girls together made for merriment below stairs.

WHAT DID THE INSPECTORS THINK OF LAMBROOK IN 1931?

Board of Education inspectors spent two days at Lambrook and the school was "recognised as efficient". The report was blandly approving:

"Mr. Cameron seems to have a flair for selecting presentable and keen young assistants."

"This school is unusual in that the work is set out in a written syllabus."

"The classics here are better taught than in any Preparatory School I have visited."

Their comments revealed the liveliness of the common room and perhaps a hint of surprise that no one was 'crammed' with extra tuition. The results came from superb grounding.

"There are some points in which the school does not accord with the views of progressive educationists but on the whole it is a case of leaving well alone."

This faint praise was regarded as an accolade by the two headmasters who would sooner have died than be thought progressive ! The grossest insult Archie could muster for a school was "I'm sure they're very good at Greek dancing and tree climbing!"

WHAT DID THE BOYS
THINK OF IT – THEN OR LATER ?

Charles Clarke, Andrew Mayes, Derek Peck and Roy Redgrave were all boys at Lambrook in the 1930s and had sons there in the 1970s.

"Basically Lambrook has altered very little... and when so many values and concepts have changed, this, I think, is no bad thing."   JDWP

"Who in the 1930s would have dreamed of the scientific and technological advances which are accepted as normal now? Lambrook's beliefs, aims, education and standards have remained, but the way they are achieved has altered."   CMAM

"There never seemed any time to do anything except what had to be done and there was only just time to do that.... Bad work was rewarded more severely years ago... Everybody loved Gerald Chamberlain but they took advantage of the kindliness of his nature. Equally they had a high regard for Jim Rankin although they knew that any departure from the highest standard would result in instant correction. Brian Bentley has been a tower of strength to us all... A very high standard of cricket manners, both on and off the field, was insisted on by Guy Cameron. The influence of Archie Forbes, with his Labradors and flicking fingers, and of Guy Cameron, with his trim figure and dry smile, was immense."   CNC

"Lessons were made interesting and time passed quickly but prep in the schoolroom (now the dininghall) really was a misery. The lighting was poor, it was cold, and there were tables and irregular verbs to learn. How could you concentrate when the illustrious fathers of some boys at school today were flicking paper balls at you ? Current affairs, taught by Phil Squarey were always a highlight, based on the excellent reportage of Picture Post. We were encouraged to keep scrap books and to read the papers. It made us feel much less cut off from the world outside. When the going got rough there was a gnarled old fellow who listened to a small boy's miseries and would grunt inarticulate advice. His name was Mr.Funnel and he cleaned shoes in a tin lean-to near the changing room. There seemed to be nothing he was not interested in – he might, I now suspect, have been very deaf!"   RMFR

WHAT MIGHT TODAY'S BOYS THINK OF
LAMBROOK IN THE 1930s?

Lambrook was very crowded then with 88 boys and no Westfield. There were two dormitories on the upper floor of the classroom block, 13 boys slept at Orchard House and 9 at Brook Cottage (The Bungalow). The Library was also the form room of the top form who guarded their territory jealously so that juniors chose books in haste. Two classes worked in the schoolroom, divided by a curtain – an arrangement hated by boys and masters. There was little opportunity for a boy to be quiet or on his own and, as Roy Redgrave said feelingly, nowhere to sit except on a hard, hard bench.

The boys were similarly restricted outside too. Until the hay was cut in the long field they could not play there but had to go in single file to the cricket field. Long break in the summer was devoted to net practice for most, swimming lessons for some and only a few were really free. Only senior boys were allowed tennis rackets (there were two grass courts) and not until cricket matches had ended because boys who did not handle a cricket ball regularly would never develop the skills of spin bowling. Dozens of boys, bowling to oak trees, learned to turn the ball cunningly.

Cricket was very important and had many facets. Every boy was taught to score and prizes were given for well kept scorebooks. Dab crick-

ORCHARD HOUSE
Built by E.D.Mansfield in 1898 as a sanatorium, Orchard House has accommodated Lambrook boys and masters and their families for a century.

et was played avidly in old scorebooks: one boy alone could have a satisfying innings by Hutton or Bradman against Mussolini's bowling or two boys could play a whole match between fantastic teams often with themselves in star roles. Pulpit cricket (scoring the preacher's mannerisms) could be played with folded hands and an angelic expression. French cricket was played with half a bat and any old ball, and Stone Pitch was a marvellous game for any number of boys and masters in the corner of the playground between two buildings. Owzat was in vogue too. It consisted of two small metal hexagons, like sections of a pencil: one had figures for runs on its sides and the other had LBW, Bowled, Caught etc. Bowler and batsman rolled them alternately, totting up huge numbers of runs and fallen wickets. Cricket took its toll from free time too: groups of boys rolled the centre square with the heavy horse roller. One farmer's son hated cricket, hated the centre square and hated this chore. He planned a splendid revenge, sprinkling turnip seed surreptitiously in front of the roller. To his sorrow it never came up.

In the winter, break was spent in the playground (larger then, with no artroom and no assembly hall). Mouldy Line was played by boys and masters. One "he" started by catching someone, they joined hands and caught more. As the line grew longer, taunted by cries of "Mo-ou-ldy Li-ine", the agile few found it difficult to escape. By the Chapel door was the stump of a huge tree with a seat round it. The Mouldy Line flowed over this obstacle like a tidal wave.

Phil Squarey coached the rugger three quarters in break in the playground: they ran to and fro passing the ball and dodging both the Mouldy Line and its escapers. After practising in these conditions the three quarters found opposing teams easy meat. The noise was tremendous with the Mouldy Line shouting directions to its two ends, taunts from those still free and bellows of "PASS" from Phil Squarey. The duty master's stentorian "ALL IN" when the clock struck could hardly be heard.

The Lambrook Electrical Club flourished with Jumbo Chamerlain's help. Boys huddled over crystal sets on the touchline and broadcast match commentaries to the laundry maids. Andrew Hake, Alistair Henderson and John Stuart Shepherd were the founder members. The Lambrook Flying Club, complete with windsleeve, flew balsa wood Frog aeroplanes, powered by twisted rubber bands, all over the cricket field. Planes often stuck in trees and a master or Harry the groundsman had to be inveigled into retrieving them.

The Punic Wars were refought with gusto in the 1930s. Rome was built mainly of hay between the wire fence and a hawthorn tree overlooking the cricket field. The Roman cohorts, and they were legion, were commanded by Ernle Bradford and Owen Hickey. Carthage was up a willow tree just across the Lamb. The Carthaginians, commanded by Lawrence Poole, were a more select band: they had to be – Carthage was distinctly cramped. Peter Rushbrooke, a Carthaginian of note, was over six feet tall aged 12. His shoes in the bootroom used to get mixed up with Archie's.

The school had access for wide games to Mr. Power's Little Wood in Cricketers' Lane and the Big Wood opposite. They also used Hill 60 at Brockhill. Guy Cameron's birthday coincided with Guy Fawkes and was truly celebrated. Occasionally the outsize guy was pulled in the pony trap by the Scouts to be ceremonially burned in the gravel pit at Hayley Green so that the village could enjoy it too.

A popular book read aloud on Sunday evenings was *Vice Versa* by Anstey in which Mr. Bultitude, a fat businessman, changes places with his son, returning to a harsh life at school. If today's Lambrook boy went back to the '30s he would find a more spartan though a kindly regime. With little free time and few places to spend it, two activities which loomed large were the boys' story competition and the plays. Five plays were written by Guy Roberts, with music by Archie Forbes and elaborate electrics by Jumbo Chamberlain and the Electrical Club. *Sunset at dawn* in 1935 had a cast of 39 boys. The boys' stories were written in free time by individuals or by pairs. In 1934 no fewer than 68 of the 75 boys wrote 40 stories between them. The seven defaulters may have been too busy with Dinky toys which were popular this year, but story writing was voluntary and it is impressive that so many completed their stories.

Probably today's boys would be most surprised at the time spent in the sickroom with flu and mumps in 1931, flu and measles in 1932, whooping cough in 1933, chicken pox in 1934, whooping cough in 1935, measles in

PLAYING STONE PITCH
C.A.C. Wilson, Guy Roberts and G.M.D. Cotterell playing Stone Pitch.
This door was by the schoolroom (now the dininghall).

1936, flu again in 1937 when "mumps ruined the football", whooping cough in 1938 and mumps and german measles in 1939. One public school headmaster wrote "a preparatory school not having an epidemic in the spring term is not doing its job properly." Lambrook was doing its job all right but Oh! how much work and worry lie behind those few words.

ABOUT THE MASTERS

Before lunch on Sundays the masters used to go to drinks at Orchard House. They seemed numerous, immensely tall, half of them smoking pipes, all talking at once and laughing about A.J.Wentworth, a hopeless assistant master whose exploits were serialised in Punch.

Apocryphal stories abound of prep schools in the '30s. Masters, thankful for any post, were sent by Messrs Grabitall and Sing to teach every subject and do duty round the clock while the affluent headmaster collected lovely lolly from parents too idle to concern themselves about their sons. Lambrook fitted this picture in only two respects: the masters worked hard (as did the two headmasters) and the fees – £60 per term – were thought high but good value for excellent teaching and all round care. Certainly Lambrook attracted lively masters: there was a sparkle of camaraderie in the common room atmosphere.

Mrs.Trimmings, the gardener's wife, looked after four masters who had rooms at Brockhill. She was a small whirlwind of a woman, washing everything in sight, and though kindhearted, she made the masters' lives a purgatory of cleanliness. Jim Rankin's window above the front door gave him an earful of two daily dramas. Summer and winter, Mrs.Trimmings scrubbed the front doorstep and the three paving slabs to the front gate. She sang merrily the while and, being deaf, her voice was not her strong point in the accepted sense. Jim Rankin would just be drifting off to sleep again when the postman measured his length on the icy path. What the postman said to himself and to Mrs.Trimmings (who heard selectively and took it as a compliment) banished sleep from the entire household. It happened regularly. When the masters asked Mrs.Trimmings if she could possibly do something else at that hour and wash the front path later, she roared with laughter and dug them in the ribs as though they had made the joke of all time. Sometimes, rushing off to school breakfast with an armful of exercise books, they forgot the icy path and crashed in their turn. Mrs.Trimmings took this as a further joke and a compliment to her cleanliness.

Two masters, Brown and Watson, left in 1935 to start their own school. As a headmaster, did George Watson have time for high jump? He could clear almost his height from an almost standing start. What a pity if no boys at Birchfield, Tettenhall learned this easy movement from him. John Roebuck, an Old Boy, came back in 1934 to teach classics and take the scouts. He was much missed when he joined the navy in 1940. It was hoped he would return after the war but he was ordained and became a parish priest.

When Jim Rankin was appointed in 1935 to teach senior maths, little did anyone realise what he would encompass in the next 37 years. He was already a good schoolmaster: he became superb and more will be written of him later. In 1937 he persuaded the headmaster to allow an extra daily period of maths for those boys in Remove who were aiming for the Navy via Dartmouth. Forty years later that period of specialist maths was still called "The Non Greeks" in deference to its humble origin. By then the classics had almost been eclipsed by the rising star of science and computer based learning.

In 1936 Lambrook went to see the funeral procession of King George V in Windsor. A first floor room with a balcony above Barber's, the antique shop, was booked and from this vantage point the boys happily counted the people who fainted and were handed over the heads of the tightly packed crowds to the First Aiders in the rear. Lambrook's hero of the day was Donald Gray, a 12 year old American who had the foresight to put a new film into his Brownie box camera and snapped off all eight exposures. Few boys had cameras then but fewer still would have used a whole film in one go. He had not watched any of the procession but he alone had a splendid record of it. Some masters said dismissively "How like an American" but once his film was developed they were full of admiration.

In 1937 not only was Monopoly invented, taking Lambrook by storm, but Brian Bentley joined the staff. He was later acknowledged in the prep school world to be the best French teacher this side of La Manche. In the '30s, French was almost as dead a language as Latin. Brian transmitted his love of France in a lively manner – a novel approach. He was a nimble tap-dancer and, though shy, could be persuaded to take his square of lino to the end of term staff meeting and, with Archie at the piano, enlivened matters most pleasantly.

The spring of 1937 was the wettest in living memory and these young masters probably cursed the rain which curtailed the training of teams on the soggy fields. Always dry was Mr.Power's field which the school rented for fifty years before buying it. Walks were a dreary alternative. Senior boys led the walk and a master brought up the rear. Archie regularly took the Sunday walk and told splendid stories. Flora Forbes knew as they passed Orchard House if the story was good. If it was really exciting, 40 or 50 boys would walk backwards, the better to lip read if they were out of earshot. When they reached the boothole door with two minutes to go, they might hear the Thrilling Conclusion or the dread words "To Be Continued", greeted with a groan of "OOOH, SIR."

1938 was the year of Munich and the *Chronicle* recorded "intense thankfulness. We came back in September under the shadow of impending war. Gas masks and trench digging brought home what the reality would be like and the disorganisation even in our own little community doesn't bear thinking about. It was an intense relief when the nations of Europe, having looked over the brink of the pit, shrank back. We must hope that the trench which now adorns the top field will be of use only to remind us of a terribly anxious time. It is devoutly to be hoped that such a time will never recur and that casualty lists like those of 1914 – 1918 will never again have to become a feature of the *Chronicle*."

Meanwhile Guy Cameron's health was causing concern and reluctantly he decided to retire. He was 46. His 1916 wound had never healed in spite of several operations. It was incredible that he had managed to cope with the demands of school life and even take part in Cricket Weeks. Hardly anyone knew that he still had an open wound in his side. Owen Hickey remembered Guy as "a serene and humorous companion. He had a breadth of sympathy which enabled him to see a value in people whom others might overlook, and an unassumed modesty which reconciled him to the quiet occupations of his retirement – a routine office job during the war, gardening which he had never given a thought to before, and the ordinary round of village life."

December 1939 was the date agreed for the handover, when the Cameron family would retire to their cottage near Bideford and the Forbes family would move into Lambrook. Little did anyone know what a momentous date – the declaration of war on 3rd September 1939 – would intervene. Amid these world changing events it is reassuring to read that "the

Scouts with Jim Rankin built a particularly fine rope bridge across the Lamb this year."

A DIGRESSION ON EPIDEMICS

THE INFECTIOUS ILLNESSES OF CHILDHOOD have been almost banished since the early years of the century. It was then thought necessary to avoid infection by keeping the community as closed as possible. This meant that an epidemic, when it came, was likely to be a big one. *The Chronicles* between 1910 and 1930 reveal this:

"The summer term was much interfered with by chicken pox. Some 30 boys revelled in the disease. Few were really ill and none caused any anxiety but it was annoying! No Parents' Day and no matches till towards the end of term"

"Four boys returned with slight coughs and before long we were indulging freely in whooping cough. This entirely spoilt the whole term, work and games."

"A new boy broke out with measles ten days after our return. This spelt ruination for the term's work and games and we would draw a veil over the whole thing."

During the 1880s, boys who lived near enough were allowed home for a half term exeat, according to Audley Gray, "but far too many boys contracted epidemic diseases which wrecked the rest of term so this concession was finally withdrawn."

Orchard House had been built as the school sanatorium in 1898 but was used mainly to accommodate masters. C.L.Norris Elye had scarlet fever his first term in 1898 and spent six weeks at Orchard House with two nurses from the Princess Christian Nursing Home in Windsor. They were paid £3 a week

each, he said, and his father thought this a great deal of money. Schools liked to boast a separate sanatorium but in fact they were of limited use. Brook Cottage was called the Sanatorium during the 1930s but was seldom used as such.

Visiting during term time was minimal. F.D.Browne wrote:

"Only two boys went outside the gates and as these fell victim first and practically on the same day, we are not sure to whom we are indebted for spoiling the term. This only emphasises how careful one has to be in keeping to the rule that no one goes out except under the most exceptional circumstances."

"This is the main reason why we do not go out in term time. Most parents are kind enough not to ask that their sons should be allowed to do so, and we are grateful to them for helping us to keep the place as free of infection as possible."

Each boy brought back to school a Health Certificate signed by his parents saying that "he has no symptoms of the common cold and has not been in contact with infectious illness during the previous three weeks." This meant in effect that he had not been to a party or an indoor entertainment during that time.

It is easy now to regard these precautions as pernickety but illnesses considered slight today were often serious before World War 1. During Mr. Browne's first ten years as headmaster, no fewer than six of his young Old Boys died between the ages of 14 and 18. One had measles at his public school, was visited by his anxious mother, who also caught measles and both died. *The Chronicles* carry the obituaries of these young Old Boys and often express relief

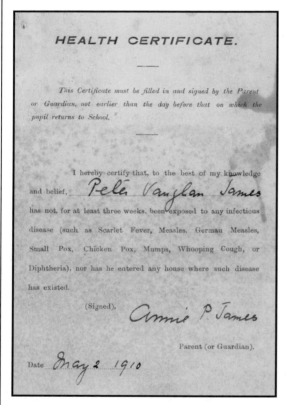

HEALTH CERTIFICATE.

This Certificate must be filled in and signed by the Parent or Guardian, not earlier than the day before that on which the pupil returns to School.

I hereby certify that, to the best of my knowledge and belief, *Peter Vaughan James* has not, for at least three weeks, been exposed to any infectious disease (such as Scarlet Fever, Measles, German Measles, Small Pox, Chicken Pox, Mumps, Whooping Cough, or Diphtheria), nor has he entered any house where such disease has existed.

(Signed), *Annie P. James*

Parent (or Guardian).

Date *May 2 1910*

that someone had pulled through a serious illness. The King nearly died from appendicitis at this time. Anxious indeed were the long days and nights of nursing.

They were not only anxious but very hard work. The school nurse became the commanding officer with agency nurses to assist. Mrs.Forbes helped when the whole top floor became a hospital with 30 or 40 boys in bed.

First they needed nursing, then amusing with quiet occupations in bed for a few more days and finally supervising during several days of convalescence.

Food, medicines, books, toys, even coal for the open fires had to be carried up to the fourth floor and then round a remarkably inconvenient building. The service lift, installed in 1930, proved a blessing. Food arrived hot and even the heavy coal buckets could be pulled up on it. When a sickroom had to be kept warm at night, pieces of coal were wrapped separately in newspaper so the night nurse could put them on the fire quietly without dirtying her hands. Going to sleep by flickering firelight was a delight which today's young will never know.

The policy of avoiding infection continued right through the '20s and '30s. Families with sons at prep school usually had domestic help at home so mothers could avoid taking children shopping. Woolworths and the cinema were thought to be hotbeds of infection. The nanny grapevine meant that children were kept away from houses where there were coughs and colds.

World War 2 changed all this in a twinkling. Resident domestics and nannies disappeared almost overnight. Queues and crowds were unavoidable. Small children went everywhere, caught everything and were nursed by mothers and fathers who caught measles and mumps themselves when there was nobody to nurse them.

The school which could write home

saying Johnny's chickenpox had only kept him out of lessons for a couple of days was likely to be hailed as a saviour by a mother who had never had it herself and was coping with 3 year old twins and a baby. Nursing childhood infections was seen as part of the preparatory school's task in the post war years and if epidemics occurred frequently the only boys likely to succumb were a few juniors.

In the 1950s headmasters rang each other before a match if there was infectious illness in school in case the opposition wished to cancel. As attitudes slowly changed, more schools disregarded quarantines, agreeing simply that visiting teams should not go indoors. Boys healthy enough to play in matches were thought unlikely to transmit an infection.

One enlightened headmaster always replied "Thank you for ringing me – you know my motto, don't you?" His motto, "Never tell the matron" was well known among local headmasters who thought it was just his little joke. However Philip Brownless watching a match at this school once mentioned measles and realised from the horror of the headmaster's wife that it was not a joke! In 20 years of not telling the matron this man had not even told his wife that an enemy school had an infectious illness. By 1970 a group of headmasters agreed that an infection had never been introduced in this way but the information was still exchanged as visiting parents, especially expectant mothers, appreciated knowing.

Inoculations today mean that these infections, if caught at all, are much less severe. Measles, even thirty years ago, could do lasting damage and the possible complications to hearts, eyes or ears probably did not appear until the second week of illness. Two weeks in bed with anything would be astonishing now. Convalescence is similarly shortened. Any grandparent can tell of school friends who missed half a term or more with appendicitis or an infection. Car heaters too have transformed the scene since the 1960s by enabling a child to travel before he is fully fit. It was a help when a boy could sometimes go home in a heated car for a day or two.

The epidemic still viewed gravely is 'flu. Opinion fluctuates about flu jabs but three facts remain: firstly it can cause a big epidemic: secondly people can go down with it again the week after having apparently recovered: thirdly the grown ups catch it as well. Small wonder that *The Chronicle* speaks of relief that Lambrook almost avoided the epidemic of Spanish flu which caused many deaths in 1919.

The Asian flu epidemic of 1957 was hectic. It hit the grownups as suddenly and as hard as the boys. The organisation of this epidemic was Nurse Goldwin's masterpiece. The beds in Lambrook were quickly filled. Some 70 boys slept at Westfield and Orchard House and it was impossible to nurse and feed them there with so many grown ups ill. Beds were brought in tractor loads from Westfield to the Library. At one time there were 57 boys ill simultaneously and there were 91 cases in all.

Proportionately fewer boys succumbed a second time than in the public schools which was attributed to the higher staff-boy ratio in a prep school. Grownups with splitting heads tottered round on aching legs offering fluids to recumbent forms one day and found the same boys next day sitting up in bed asking plaintively "Only one sausage?"

Are there any pluses to an epidemic?

There is a lot of fun to be had when the community gets so mixed up. Boys of different ages find themselves in adjacent beds. 'Imported' nurses brought a breath of fresh air into a jaded community in the past. (In 1938 one 'imported' nurse was rumoured to have received 9 proposals from boys with measles but she married a master.) Today's emergency nursing help is likely to be provided by masters' wives. People find themselves doing strange jobs: an assistant matron or a senior boy may teach, anybody may cook and once more the headmaster's wife goes back to the washing up. There is a feeling of buoyancy, almost of heroism, among the dwindling survivors in the dininghall.

The tiny minus is the pang of envy felt when – after weeks of carrying food and medicines around sick beds, writing case notes and ringing home with bulletins, toiling up those endless stairs with comforts for the troops, after nursing domestics in other languages and masters in other houses, after broken nights and having flu themselves on their feet – Sister and the matrons hear that Mrs. X is off to a seaside hotel to convalesce after "a touch of flu." However, it is a small minus. Mrs. X did not have the satisfaction of seeing boys bouncing downstairs again in ebullient good spirits. Even the noise is a comfort to the school nurse after the uncanny quiet of ill boys. Although tired out she rejoices to hear their wonted clamour once more.

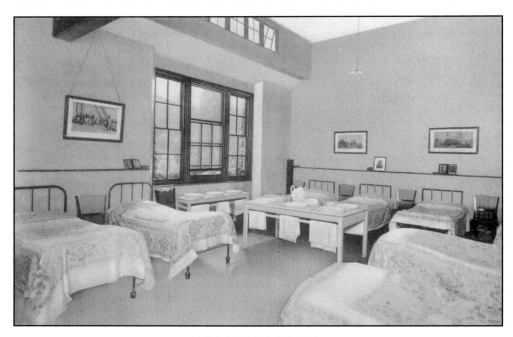

THE HARP DORMITORY

This room, in E.D. Mansfield's classroom block built in 1888, was the Harp dormitory for nearly fifty years. When the senior dormitories moved to Westfield in 1946 it became Remove classroom for nearly forty years. Since then it has been an orchestra room and a video theatre.

5

A. H. FORBES
HEADMASTER
1939–1956

THE SECOND WORLD WAR 1939–1945

ARCHIE FORBES had waited eighteen years to become sole headmaster of Lambrook but the opportunity could not have come at a worse time. Lambrook's proximity to London, hitherto an asset, now made the school's future doubtful. Winkfield Row was thought to be on the flight path of aircraft en route to bomb London. Should Lambrook move to safer quarters elsewhere? This was easily answered: big money would be needed for a move and there was none. By August 1939 share prices had fallen so steeply that Archie had to sell everything to buy out the Camerons' two thirds share. The declaration of war on that sunny Sunday 3rd September 1939 ended the stop-go hopes of preceding months. Now there was work to be done and plans to be made for coping with blackout, air raids, dwindling staff and rationing. Fresh uncertainties loomed up continually.

BLACKOUT AND AIR RAID PRECAUTIONS

Air raid precautions were put into effect at once. Sticky tape or netting was stuck over windows to minimise accidents from flying glass. Miles of black material were sewn by helpers up and down the village into curtain linings. Checking the blackout was a nightly nightmare. Curtains had to be scrupulously drawn: if a chink of light was reported by an Air Raid warden, the third offence carried a fine of £50 (about £1,200 today). Lambrook soon had two warnings so the blackout was checked by the headmaster's wife and 11 year old daughter, Rona. One waited outside in the dark while the other switched on every light in turn, listening for a shout from the lawn below, "Chink on the right" or "Crack down the middle". It took two hours.

The staff hall beside the kitchen, with its ceiling reinforced by tree trunks, was equipped as a night shelter with tiers of bunks. The changing room had to be gas proofed, with air traps and gas traps and specially papered ceiling. The experts also insisted on a daytime shelter so a zigzag trench was dug in the top field, lined with sandbags and covered with earth and turf. It was never used and eventually became a giant sand heap. However, no one dared disregard the experts: though the signposts had been removed, the milestone still said "25 miles to Hyde Park Corner".

Sleeping arrangements were reorganised. The top floor was vulnerable so sickrooms and dormitories moved downstairs. The library became a dormitory. The headmaster's family quarters on the first floor were the obvious place for sick boys so they need not move during air raids. The Forbes family moved to the top floor but with air raids and fire watching they seldom had a proper night in bed until the holidays. At first the boys slept upstairs and came down to the basement when the siren went. This was frightening and disrupted everyone's sleep so a different system evolved. The boys got ready for bed upstairs but came down just before lights out, settling into their bunk beds calmly as a routine. The hay fever boys slept on air mattresses on the kitchen floor.

GUNS AND BOMBS

There were anti-aircraft guns nearby so the bangs and crumps were often loud. In a noisy raid, Archie would read a story aloud by torchlight. When the crumps were frighteningly near he administered what he called Air Raid Pills. These were boiled sweets carefully hoarded by Flora. Tooth decay seemed less important than calm sleep. Nicholas Rivett Carnac remembers the stories and the sweets and the quiet assurance of the grown ups enabling the youngsters to take it all in their stride.

Bombers being chased by fighter planes often jettisoned their bombs on open country for greater speed. In one bad night, 200 bombs fell between Bracknell and Ascot. Another night, a stick of five bombs was dropped across the Lambrook fields, straddling the pavilion and Orchard House without damaging either. One fell in the field behind the cricket nets and one in front of the pavilion where the ground is still slightly humped. The next fell in the Orchard House drive, half on the grass and half on the gravel, and another in the rose garden by the Orchard House tennis court. The two ends of the yew hedge enclosing the rose garden stuck straight up in the air on either side of the bomb crater. One boy in Orchard House slept right through the noise, saying afterwards that he thought he had heard a door bang! Flora's ducks in the orchard were just coming into lay but the fright put them off. They were not the only ones frightened: a week later another bomb fell in the orchard but without exploding, so the housemaster and his wife escorted the boys up to Lambrook to spend the rest of the night on the drawing room floor. The boys enjoyed diversions from routine but Archie said the staff badly needed a couple of calming whiskeys. Orchard House boys were envied as they could sometimes collect souvenirs on their way to breakfast.

The biggest bomb fell in the Westfield field, not then part of the school. This 500 pounder, then thought huge, fell at 9.30 pm with a tremendous whistling noise, breaking all the windows on the south and west sides of Lambrook and Westfield. It has caused trouble ever since as it shook both buildings so badly.

THE HOME GUARD

Road blocks – tree trunks fixed to big iron wheels – were set up ready to be pulled across the road to delay invaders. High powered officials from the War Office came to decide the best positions for them and the sand-bagged emplacements from which the Home Guard would defend them.

One was sited between Lambrook's two big gates. Any sensible Germans would have driven in at the front gate and out at the back. They would then have missed the Home Guard who lay in wait, two at a time, watching the road through the Lambrook fence, hoping Mrs. Forbes would creep out in the dark with a thermos of cocoa for them. Everyone had bottles of rusty nails and tin tacks ready to throw down ahead of the invaders' tyres.

ARCHIE FORBES

Archie only did Home Guard duty during the holidays but several masters, notably Phil Squarey and Jim Rankin, served in term time as well. In the holidays, mock battles were keenly fought between the Winkfield and Winkfield Row platoons. Winkfield boasted an armoured car: actually it was Phil Squarey's Ford V8 which he sent away to have an extra layer of bodywork added. The 4 inch gap thus created had to be filled with gravel to make it bullet proof but the car was then so heavy it could hardly climb Brockhill so they emptied the gravel out again. However it was deemed invincible in local manoeuvres though there was no ammunition for test-ing. It had a turret for a machine-gun but as no machine-gun was forth-coming in spite of appeals to the War Office and, as the chap in the turret couldn't see anything, they drove about turret-less. A man in a tin hat (yes, they had several of those) with his head sticking up through a hole in the roof, stood shaking a cocoa tin full of stones, shouting "You're dead" to the Winkfield Row platoon. They weren't allowed to shoot him with their wooden rifles because, of course, he was in a bullet-proof turret.

Winkfield Row, outclassed in the matter of equipment by Winkfield who had several pairs of boots and a pair of binoculars, were responsible for guarding the telephone exchange opposite the White Horse. The village

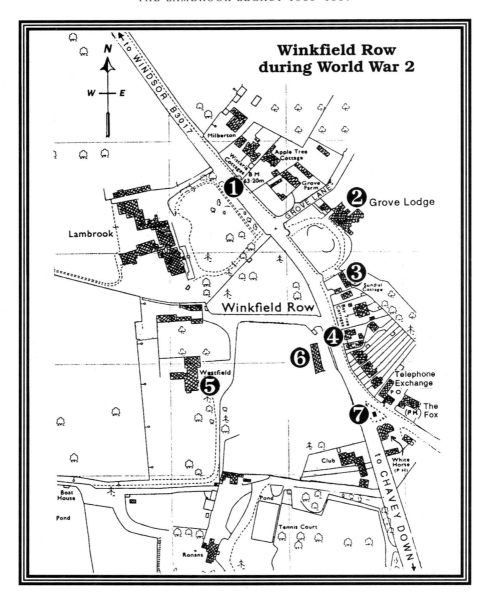

Winkfield Row during World War 2

considered it the nerve centre for which the Germans would aim on their way to London. A strong point was constructed for its defence on the tiny green in the middle of the road junction, built of wooden boxes filled with sand. Archie, who felt the cold terribly, hated his turns on night duty surrounded by boxes saying "Lily bulbs – keep cool".

DWINDLING STAFF

Four young masters soon had their call up papers for the forces, Brian Bentley (French), Teddy Duckett (Music), John Roebuck (Classics) and A.R. Williams (Maths). Schoolmasters over 35 were a reserved occupation. Jim Rankin's 35th birthday made him a test case while the War Office debated for 18 months: his papers came when he was nearly 37. Although fit, he found it tough doing square bashing and assault courses with 18 year olds. Harry Birch, groundsman for 15 years, was a big loss and so was Mr. Swanborough, 'Carpenter'. The delightful Welsh maids melted away to munitions factories or work 'of national importance'. Laura Bullimore was the sole survivor of the quintet in the laundry. Miss Hordern, matron, and Miss Williams, housekeeper, who had battled with rationing, were called up for the women's services. Of the four outside men, only Ted Coxhead and George Trimmings, both veterans, were left to cope with playing fields, vegetable gardens and stoking eight coke fired boilers.

The gaps left were hard to fill. Older men came to teach and some were distinctly odd. One finally admitted that he had come hoping there would be more food in a community! He liked four spoonfuls of sugar in his tea. After polite requests to take less had proved useless, Flora showed him four ounces of sugar in a jam jar, his ration for a week for cooking as well as in tea. He was amazed that Flora was not going to allow him to eat into the boys' ration after finishing his own. He left as soon as he thought he had found somewhere more comfortable to spend the war. Sometimes the tide of war washed back old friends like the Rev. Reginald Clough. The Crawshaws also rejoined the staff when their south coast school was requisitioned. Miss Pim, a wonderful teacher, came during the war's coldest winter wearing layers of cardigans and everyone counted her different coloured necklines daily as a sort of weather forecast. They all gave time

WINKFIELD DURING WORLD WAR 2

1. *The road block to prevent or delay invaders getting to London was sited by the War Office experts between Lambrook's two gates.*

2. *Grove Lodge, then one huge house, was the wartime home of the 9 year old King Feisal of Iraq and his mother with their entourage. The Iraqi soldiers who did sentry duty at each gate were an endless source of fascination to the village.*

3. *The Home Guard Platoon Headquarters. Sgt. A.H.Forbes spent the night here on 20 September 1940 priming grenades with the postman who was so nervous his hands shook. AHF later said nothing he had done in World War 1 had been half so dangerous.*

4. *This was a sweetshop which closed in 1939. It was probably here that Lambrook boys in the 1870s used to buy sweets "at a little shop almost opposite the school gate".*

5. *Westfield's owners moved away in 1939 and the house became a store for the duration of the war.*

6. *Luxurious kennels built in the 1930s for their prize winning greyhounds by the owners of Westfield.*

7. *The strong point built of bulb boxes on the little green at the road junction was to defend the telephone exchange. The Post Office was a small shop until the 1960s.*

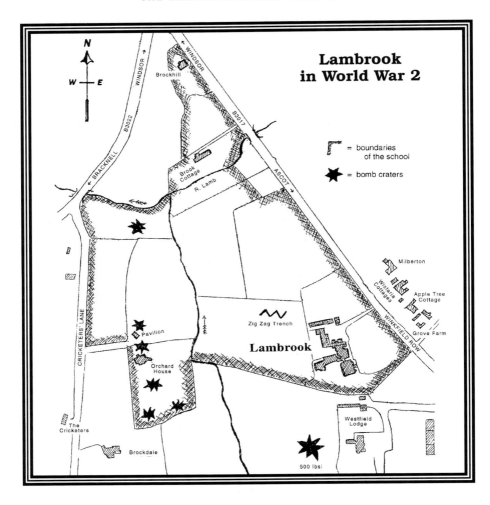

to ARP duties and the dreaded fire watching. One master used to walk down from Brockhill wearing his gas mask to keep the dank night air out of his bronchial tubes. It was a relief that he never met a trigger happy Home Guard on a dark night. In one short year, Archie at 40 found himself one of the younger masters. Enthusiasm, energy and fun became increasingly valuable as people became increasingly tired.

Another loss was Handley, the chef, whom everyone liked. His call up was deferred because he had only one eye. One evening in June 1940, Trimmings the gardener rushed into the study saying "Come quickly, Handley's had an accident on his way home." Flora and the housekeeper dashed up the road to find Handley dead, having crashed his motor bike into the back of a stationary army lorry parked outside the Jolly Gardener (now called Stirrups). In the blackout, only dim lights were allowed and

Handley had failed to see the camouflaged lorry in the bright moonlight. Having done what little they could – the first time these First Aiders had felt for a pulse in vain – they drove on to break the news to young Mrs. Handley in Slough. After crawling late to bed they had to get up early to cook school breakfast. They cooked for 100 during the next weeks, rushing through their other work and wondering how long they could keep up the pace. They also had to find time to advertise, to furnish quarters for a new cook, and to interview candidates, meeting and returning them to the station each time and trying to appear unhurried and welcoming.

FIRE WATCHING

The worst chore of all was fire watching. An incendiary bomb in a noisy raid could have set the whole building ablaze unless spotted quickly. The staff took three hour shifts at night patrolling every half hour. Archie always did till midnight. The midnight to 3 am and the 3 to 6 am shifts were shared out with Archie and Flora taking as many turns as the rest. This routine was gruelling, particularly for Archie who could never go to bed early. Grim too were the nights when Flora's turn was from midnight to 3 am and Archie's from 3 to 6 am. Some nights he only had three hours in bed.

Later they got a night watchman but he was a mixed blessing. Mr. B.'s task was to clean the boys' shoes between his tours of the building but when the shoes were still muddy in the morning, suspicions grew. In 1944 when raids seemed over, Archie and Flora went to Devon for the wedding of his god daughter, Anne Cameron. Although Mr B. was expecting them back in the small hours, he was so fast asleep they could not wake him and had to climb in through a window in their wedding finery. Next day Archie sent for Mr. B. who blustered and threatened to resign. When Archie replied "Thank you very much, Mr. B., I think that is the wise thing to do and I accept your resignation", Mr. B. was astonished and took umbrage. Thereafter he cut the family dead unless taken unawares. If greeted unexpectedly as he made stately progress through the village on his high and mighty bicycle, he would reply with a smile and "Good morning" before wobbling violently as he remembered that he Wasn't Speaking.

WAR ON THE HOME FRONT

Flora found unexpected sources of food. Cafes in Windsor were allocated rations proportionate to their pre-war needs but now had few customers. For six years Flora made a weekly trip for what one cafe called "The Elbert". This huge tray of sponge was covered from prying eyes on the back seat of the little Morris 8 and the boys devoured it gratefully, sometimes as cake, sometimes as trifle and sometimes as pudding with jam sauce. The village grapevine told of Women's Institute jam which had failed the Ministry of Food's setting tests. The WI had a sugar ration for preserving soft fruit either bottled or as jam, and naturally tried to stretch the precious sugar as far as possible. If the jam did not set properly, it could only be sold to schools for immediate consumption. When the village shop closed, Flora bought huge jars of sweets and hid them away for later. On hearing that the BeeZeeBee factory had fewer catering customers since the bombing of Slough she hurried there to buy huge tins of honey.

A tradesman's bicycle with a vast square basket proved to be worth its considerable weight and Flora regularly did the eight miles to Bracknell and back. Once the fishmonger rang to say "I've got some kippers but not enough to sell in the shop. You can have 50 pairs if you'll collect them today." They were unwrapped due to the paper shortage and every dog in Bracknell trotted behind her bicycle sniffing. Because shops in wartime had little to sell, they opened at odd times and the prudent housewife, especially if she had 80 children to feed, went shopping often so as not to miss an unexpected delivery. The petrol ration was meagre but school had an extra allowance of three gallons per month and a can of petrol was kept hidden ready to take a boy to hospital in emergency.

A farmer friend at Brockhill was not licensed to sell milk but knew that Flora needed extra for convalescent boys. They arranged a telephone code so Flora knew when to bicycle up after dark with a small churn hidden in the deep basket. Since this was on the shady side of the law, no one else could be asked to fetch it, nor could it appear as EXTRA MILK in the school accounts. It was called MANURE which Archie said disappeared just as quickly without trace. When boys had whooping cough which often made them sick, the best time to give a small meal was immediately after a bout of coughing. Having milk and eggs ready upstairs to make a quick snack was almost a lifesaver. So that not a drop of milk should be wasted in the dining hall, it became the custom for boys to turn their empty mugs upside down on their plates after the meal.

Cooked breakfast was preceded by porridge or cereal and followed by bread and marmalade when each boy had his daily butter ball. There was margarine (wartime margarine was poor stuff compared with today's) for those who wanted more bread but it was important that no one should go without his meagre butter ration. Boys' tea was also a cooked meal, followed by bread and various spreads, and then fresh fruit. A wise pantry man saw the boys cutting their apples extravagantly: if the knives were removed when they finished their bread, he thought they might eat more of the fruit. This ruse worked and the volume of apple cores dropped by half. An RAF father brought a bunch of bananas in 1943 and Archie made a comical ceremony of peeling and dividing them among about thirty boys who had never seen them before. Oranges were for Saturday nights because shirts and jerseys were just going to the wash. Matron had plenty to say when the boys had oranges one Sunday tea time. Figs were a rarity, a treat for some but not for Tim W. who protested "Nobody at home eats

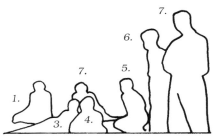

1. Flora Forbes
2. Alison Williams
3. John Fisher
4. Guy Gammell
5. Harry Birch
6. Robin Thursby Pelham
7. Tony Crawshaw

figs, not even the dog!"

Individual boys had their own garden plots and cheerful squads were deployed for tasks in the grounds as well as planting potatoes and harvesting on nearby farms. The ICI farm at Jealott's Hill asked Lambrook to help with what sounded an important contribution to their research. With the boys lined up in rows full of patriotic fervour, a carefully measured turf was turned up in front of each and he was asked to count the wire worms in it. Did it mark a turning point in the war? Archie only hoped it was worth the effort needed to get 60 boys four miles each way on foot and in relays in the little Morris.

JOURNEYS TO SCHOOL

Wartime journeys were awful with delays the only certainty. A few boys came by car, sharing with others. Buses were possible for some but their luggage had to follow by train. Passenger trains were often shunted into sidings and held up, sometimes for hours, while troop trains took priority. Station names had been removed and blackout meant gloomy waiting rooms and extremes of cold or fug in crowded carriages. Refreshments were uncertain so boys arrived tired, cold, hungry, dirty, and not infrequently with nits, which then caused more fuss than today. Two brothers after a long journey arrived with nits in their hair. On the telephone that evening their horrified mother exclaimed "But any of us might have them!" Archie, tired and for once inattentive, replied "Yes, I expect you have!"

The beginning of term was hectic. Parents sent fruit and eggs and jam and also outgrown clothes. Everything had to be swiftly stowed into labelled lockers before the siren blared its warning. Gas masks and mackintoshes had to be quickly available. Once the boys were safely in bed, Archie telephoned many parents. A boy going to boarding school anticipated the adventure with mingled pleasure and anxiety. His family, also keyed up, had the anxiety without the pleasure and sometimes needed reassurance. Major C. evidently didn't: on his third son's entry form under the heading *Any other illnesses* he put "Can't stand still and won't shut doors."

Routine, a confidence builder in itself, was difficult to sustain. Fathers and brothers were being called up, mothers were doing war work, homes were bombed or evacuated, and lives uprooted. Trains were irregular and buses scarce, so parents visited when they could, often turning up unexpectedly. It was a relief to find the boys well and busy. Mrs. D. arrived with only an hour between trains to tell her sons that their father had been killed. As she had to dash away so quickly, Flora took the two boys out on bicycles for a picnic to give them time away from school to take in the news.

Mrs. K. was stuck in India and did not see her 9 year old till he was 13. Flora, sad that Mrs. K. was missing so much of his young life, wrote weekly letters to supplement his scanty ones. Often the schoolboy letters consisted of a few scores and dramatic pictures of "Me in my bunk" and "Lambrook's bomb crater". Johnnie K, a delightful scatterbrain who also scattered his possessions, was the demon bowler of the Under 11 Cricket XI, for whom a match was a big event. He had lost his cricket shoes and Flora would not lend him someone else's which he might also lose, so he went in his walking shoes and did surprisingly well. Afterwards Flora asked him how he managed and if he had slipped badly. With a grin he said "I bowled in my socks: as you weren't there to see, I took my shoes off and gave them to the umpire to hold!"

There was once a master who died refereeing a football match. Mr. Vipan came in 1944 when his skill and energy were most needed. He ran down the field but when play surged back again the spectators saw that he had fallen. Nurse Goldwin ran and knelt beside him. He was already dead

1. D.C. Hugonin
2. Furnivall
3. Lionel Wix
4. Durnford
5. A.P. Clarke
6. F.P. Brooke Popham
7. Watson

Note the window at left shuttered as part of gas proofing the changing room.

but she wanted it to look as if he had only fainted. Half time was called early and the match moved to another ground to keep the teams and spectators occupied at a distance. Death was all too close to wartime children and it was felt important to shield the boys somewhat from this death in their midst. During the interminable wait for a suitable vehicle, Nurse Goldwin and Flora – truly a bodyguard – crouched beside him as though doing first aid. Next morning the boys were told that Mr. Vipan had not recovered and the choir later sang at his funeral in Winkfield Church. He was a fine man, sadly missed.

The soccer XI had a needle match against Ludgrove and much depended upon Stephen Wills. After the victory, the jubilant team said to Archie "Your prayer was answered, Sir!" He was mystified till he looked up the prayer he had used in Chapel that morning: "Strengthen our wills, O Lord that we may ..."

NEW BOYS AND A DAY IN BED

A new boy usually settled in easily but after a few busy days, with activities following fast upon each other from 7 am to 7 pm, a break with extra sleep was valuable. The dining hall atmosphere was like a birthday party three times a day, exhilarating but wearing. Upstairs, bath time could no longer be as gracious or leisurely as at home and the school nurse (known as Sister), however kindly she anointed his hurts or read to him, appeared a fleeting figure to be shared with many others. A day in bed showed him that Sister was always there and that being one of a select few was very pleasant. Sister would tell several, usually two per dormitory, to stay in bed next morning. They had breakfast in bed and played games on big plywood trays set between their beds. After lunch they had a sleep with the curtains shut. Sister uttered a warning at this stage: any Monkey Business or Fooling About and the whole exercise would be repeated the next day. Most slept for several hours. By tea time the place rang to their chatter. Bath time was leisurely and when the others came to bed they found their fellows sitting up like sleek cats with quips and gibes for those who were to stay in bed next day.

The knee hole of Archie's big desk made a snug cave for one new boy who spent much of his first week there. This was Archie's godson, brought by his mother by train from Devon, a long and difficult journey. With his father away in the army, the tearful child felt Archie was the sole link with his former world of sanity and peace. He sat under the desk drawing pictures and escorted Archie everywhere till he felt able to join the others. Another new boy who had also never seen the school before took one look and decided it was not for him. He made off down the field pursued by his athletic but distracted mama shrieking: "John, John, come back – I'VE PAID THE FEES!"

On his first evening in the dormitory one new boy watched the rest getting ready for bed and announced: "This is heaven without Sarah". Another marched sternly into the study after two days to say: "My mother thinks this is a good school and I want you to ring her up and tell her it's not – it's a very bad one!" They had a discussion which ended with Archie promising to ring the mother and the boy agreeing to give the school a bit longer trial.

HARD WORK AND SURPRISES

Archie and Flora determined that Hitler, who had messed up so much, should not prevent the youngsters in their care from having as normal a childhood and as much fun as possible. Hard work in the classroom and on the games field continued but surprises happened too.

Archie asked the headquarters of Bertram Mills circus if an elephant, which sometimes went for a walk with his keeper near Ascot, could please walk to Lambrook. They couldn't spare an elephant but were so amused by the request they sent a llama and a donkey instead. Once a siege was devised with the boys defending Lambrook from invaders who were the staff in disguise: the laundry man kindly dragged in an extra hamper containing a master and Archie invited the Fire Brigade for a practice if they would disguise a couple of masters in helmets and get them into the building. When second-hand ice skates were cheap in jumble sales in the summer, Flora accumulated 27 pairs. Hundreds of boys learnt to skate and played ice hockey whenever it froze.

They had impromptu parties too. Archie announced in tea that prep was cancelled and everyone was to appear in the school room for a party. Flora put dressing up clothes in each classroom. While the boys got ready in a happy hubbub, she helped Archie into an evening dress of his mother's to appear as Miss Hemstitch, the piano playing headmistress, who organised hilarious games. Prizes were likely to be Flora's carefully hoarded sweet ration.

The Davy fire escape was a belt with pulleys in which someone abseiled slowly – Oh, so slowly – down from a high window. More fun was a session with the fire escape chute, a canvas tunnel from a first floor window, which opened out like a slide and was stretched taut with rope handles by the first two who climbed down a knotted rope. Thereafter the descent was speedy with a commentary from Archie in the classroom, telling the crowd below who was coming next. "A distinguished Old Boy" might be one of the dogs sliding down emerging to cheers, followed by a parent described as an Airedale or a Labrador. Eager boys queued for turns. An apprehensive 9 year old came past the queue and whispered "Sir, is it voluntary?" Archie, beaming at the child, replied "Of course it's voluntary", picked him up and popped him straight into the tunnel, saying "Tuck your elbows in." The boy was so delighted with his achievement that he came upstairs again to queue for another go and another. If Archie had told him to queue with the rest his dread might have proved too great.

Once when rain stopped cricket about 100 people sheltered in the pavilion. Archie asked the wicket keeper if he minded getting wet – an unnecessary question – and then planted a cricket stump, putting half a crown (more than £5 today) down in front of it. Anyone who could throw the ball to hit the stump or the coin could keep it. This was a noisy business, punctuated by silence for each throw, and then groans or cheers. As the rain did not let up, Archie put down a pound note, remarking that a bigger target was evidently needed. Only the wicket keeper and Archie got soaked and the rest were happily engrossed as though at the circus.

At breakfast and lunch the staff ate with the boys, but high tea was taken by the master on duty who was glad to be relieved for the last ten minutes. Archie valued this time with the whole school. After a match colours might be awarded, some other effort commended, some political development might need explanation, perhaps some Old Boy had done something admirable. Reminders about good manners occurred then and if he said he was DISAPPOINTED about something the school left tea in a sober frame of mind. Sometimes he read to them: often there were discussions and boys' opinions were asked. It was a time for sharing jokes and concerns. Stories about boys and Old Boys abounded:if discreditable Archie prefaced them with "There was once a boy who shall be nameless..." which made the audience instantly attentive.

Archie was seldom taken by surprise though he often professed to be. Trouble was anticipated and defused with a word, either casually in the passage or formally in the study where, if he had to be firm when he wanted to laugh he would dive under his desk to straighten his face while pretending to knock out his pipe in the waste paper bin. Courteous to everyone, he expected them to be polite and punctual. He feigned deafness if a boy spoke to him with hands in pockets.

Sound sleep was essential in a community which worked and played hard, where solitude was rare and quiet was precious. Even 12 and 13 year old dormitory captains went to bed at 8 pm, but with the privilege of reading till later with a shaded bed head light, itself a reassurance to younger boys settling down to sleep. The custom of having senior boys as dormitory captains began in the war when an older sheepdog type was invaluable among bewildered youngsters during raids.

Riotous behaviour was not allowed indoors in the interests of safety and good manners but out of doors energy had full play with cricket, soccer and rugger coached five days a week plus some golf, tennis and swimming. On Sundays there was a time to let off steam with games like cops and robbers in the woods. The Scouts too gave the less athletic a chance to excel. When the fields were boggy and a walk seemed dull, Archie occasionally took a "frolic". Armed with a whistle he took the boys whooping and bouncing in the rain down to the boggiest bit of field and lined them up for a gruesome charge called Balaclava. On the command CHARGE they charged, yelling, till the whistle blew when they fell down flat in the mud. Variations on the theme ensured they were soon well exercised and ready for extra free time indoors. A new master watched aghast, finally enquiring "Do you mean we are ALLOWED to get the boys muddy?" It would not have been possible without good drying rooms.

FROM *THE LAMBROOK CHRONICLE*

Paper shortage reduced *The Chronicle* to a single folded sheet in 1941, but it recorded the amazing result of the village effort for the War Weapons Week fête held in the school grounds. "Much organisation of stalls and sideshows and much disorganisation of school work enabled us to raise £1,326 (over £30,000 today) in one afternoon. In fact everyone worked so hard at the fête and in the preceding fancy dress parade through the village that no work could be done afterwards till extra doses of sleep had restored the equilibrium of the school: but it was worth it!"

1942 saw the launch of the *M.V. LAMBROOK*, a cargo ship of 10,000 tons, named by one of the shipyard directors, whose son, Johnny Graham, was then at Lambrook. Correspondence and gifts passed regularly to and fro. One crew member begged his school boy correspondent to pay particular attention in French lessons: if only he had learnt French at school he would be getting on much better with the girls now. A letter from the ship's carpenter to the 10 year old Peter Bourne enjoined him never to forget that a pound note and his mother are a boy's best friends. The *M.V. LAMBROOK* survived the war in spite of damage from mines. Among several Old Boys who came in contact with the ship were Captain P.W. Brooking and Lieut. D.R.G. Goldsmith, whose destroyer escorted the

WAR WEAPONS WEEK
Procession led by Robin Thursby Pelham
advertising the War Weapons Week Fete.

Lambrook in convoy more than once.

The 1945 *Chronicle* expresses the thankfulness "shared by all who have had the care of children during these war years, coupled with deepest sympathy for the relations and friends of more than fifty Old Boys whose names are recorded in the Roll of Honour. Thankfulness looms large too that we have been able to stay in our own premises, spared many trials and horrors during these years of upheaval and suffering in the world."

VE DAY, 8th MAY, 1945

When the war ended the celebrations included a trip on the Thames for the boys, teaching and domestic staff and all their families. Fizzy pop and lemonade were rare treats which Flora had been buying for months. A convoy of taxis arrived, each member of staff escorted a group of boys by taxi to Bracknell, by train to Reading, and on foot to the steamer at Caversham. A piano had been put on board, and the housekeeper had arrived earlier in a taxi laden with hampers of food. When the steamer reached Goring, Archie took the boys to call on Tom Miller, an Old Boy newly back from POW camp. 150 people and seven dogs enjoyed this outing, planned to be as memorable as the one Archie had enjoyed as a new boy in 1907, when the whole school went for a river picnic.

VE Day began a new era. The day was marked by a service in Chapel followed by a whole holiday, with the place bedecked in flags and a bonfire in the evening. "Such a pace having been set for VE Day, it was as well that VJ Day fell in the holidays" remarked the Editor of *The Chronicle*. Lambrook had not merely survived the war but was in good fettle to tackle the problems and opportunities of the post war era. With the school full – 90 boys with a full entry book and a waiting list for terms ahead – and expecting the return of three fine pre-war masters, all was ready for embarking boldly on the next stage in a world that promised to be very different.

Years later an Old Boy who had not been back to Lambrook since World War 2 met Flora who greeted him warmly and said she felt the boys in war time had had a raw deal compared with other generations. His reply was heart warming: "Not at all: we thought you and Archie put on a jolly good show".

POSTWAR LAMBROOK
1946–1950

In May 1945 VE Day was celebrated with bonfires, church bells and village rejoicings. VJ Day in August came and went quietly but shortages continued: bread rationing began the following year. Building materials were scarce and people longed for a home of their own. The camaraderie of the war years ceased abruptly and a deep exhaustion made people bicker once they had no common enemy. There were personal adjustments to be made as the forces were demobilised, some families reunited with semi strangers and others coming to terms with gaps in the family circle.

PLANNING AHEAD

Lambrook had many needs. As well as bomb damage, the buildings were shabby, grubby and overcrowded. Archie Forbes had foreseen the coming need to accommodate married masters and had long dreamed of buying Westfield, the mansion next door to Lambrook. When his mother had died in 1940, her Camberley house was requisitioned by the Council. Archie now hoped to sell it in order to buy Westfield. However the Council put a compulsory purchase order on the Camberley house so it could only be sold to them and at their valuer's price which was one third of its market value. Protesting, Archie and his solicitor asked for an independent valuation and also that the sale might go to arbitration: neither appeal was allowed. The Council valuer admitted that the house's poor condition was due to gross neglect during the Council's full repairing tenancy! Buying Westfield in 1946 was therefore a financial headache and an act of faith.

WESTFIELD

Formerly called Westfield Lodge, this "desirable residence in Georgian style" had several cottages and 17 acres of land. During the 1920s it had briefly been the junior department of Heathfield, Ascot, an exclusive girls' school two miles up the road. Stories about Miss Wyatt, Heathfield's leg-

WESTFIELD
bought for Lambrook in 1946.

endary headmistress, were still current in 1946. Archie remembered Miss Wyatt as an imperious lady before whom not only schoolgirls trembled. Mr.Scull, who worked with a Bracknell firm of builders, remembered her telephone calls. "Mr.Scull, I want to spend two nights at Westfield: would you please send the men to move my bed ?" Four men went at once to Heathfield to dismantle the bed, take it up the road to her room at Westfield and reassemble it. At teatime came a countermanding order: "DEAR Mr.Scull, I have changed my mind. Would you please ask those NICE men to bring my bed back again ?" Her bed often travelled to and fro.

After Heathfield's brief occupancy, Westfield was bought by a family whose greyhounds lived luxuriously in a centrally heated range of kennels, with a flatlet for the kennelman at one end and a tiled kitchen at the other for preparing dog food. It was the wonder of Winkfield Row. In 1947 it was converted into two bungalows. The big house had stood empty for six years as a store and was in poor shape. Flora Forbes became clerk of the works, acquiring vast knowledge of roofs, wiring circuits and drainage systems over the whole estate.

STAFF

Now, with 14 cottages, flats and houses to offer when accommodation was desperately short, Archie built up a superb staff. Jim Rankin, Brian Bentley and Teddy Duckett all returned from the forces, a great relief. Sadly, Gerald Chamberlain, a patient kindly man who spent 21 of his 42 years at Lambrook, had died from cancer as the war ended. Phil Squarey, colourful and idiosyncratic, had dashed off for a year to the Middle East, not in the forces but "in pursuit of locusts", returning in September 1945. His absence had been as unwelcome as unexpected.

R.V. Johns was demobbed in 1944 and, resolving not to be a solicitor again, applied to teach at Lambrook. At first he was elated at being invited to an interview but then had butterflies and wondered how to get out of such a terrifying prospect. Reluctant to admit to cold feet and unable to think of an excuse, he found himself in the train to Bracknell in what he later described as a blue funk. He thought of getting out at Ascot and catching the next train back to London but missed his chance. His last hope was that whoever met him would be late so he could rush over the footbridge and leap into the Waterloo train. Once safely back in London he would phone to apologise.

However the Morris 8, with the headmaster's daughter, Isla, on her first solo run, had arrived early to allow time for planning the hill start. She was unaware of RVJ's nervousness: he was unaware of anything except his folly in coming. Once Archie had greeted him, his butterflies flew away. Later he said it was the happiest day of his life as his love affair with Lambrook never faltered. Both Lambrook and the Forbes family gained a wonderful friend. His aptitude as a kindly schoolmaster, particularly with younger boys, endeared "Daddy Johns" to generations.

INCREASING NUMBERS

In 1945 there were 90 boys and Lambrook was overcrowded. The purchase of Westfield solved several problems. The dormitories for 30 senior boys moved to Westfield which accommodated two married masters and other staff as well. In Lambrook, the Harp and the Dragon dormitories became classrooms. Never again did two different classes have to learn at opposite ends of the big schoolroom, interested only in what the master at the other end was attempting to teach. So difficult was this that Archie had sometimes taken his Latin class to the entrance hall, to test their grammar on Mount Olympus. They all sat on the bottom stair and each correct answer meant rising a step higher. A rapid fire stream of questions, matched to quick minds and slow, generated enthusiasm for Latin grammar and the unusual quiet of the schoolroom was a welcome respite for a colleague.

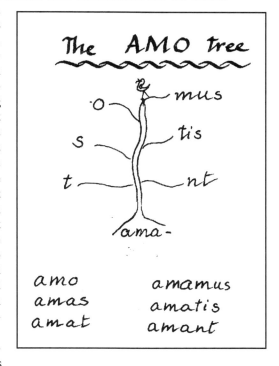

THE FIRST LATIN LESSON
from Archie Forbes.

Archie also taught Latin grammar by a method like grandmother's footsteps on the low stage in the schoolroom. The class stood in a row with toes behind a crack in the floorboards. A right answer meant moving forward one board and a "duffer" who got it wrong had to move back. "Gump!" said Archie in mock shock, dropping both corners of his mouth to make a face as he said it. The questions were preceded by the name of the boy who was to answer and as the names came in any order, everyone was alert. A grand piano stood on the stage and Christopher Eden remembered that "brilliant types like David Youngman had to move across and squeeze past the piano as their scores rose."

A WAITING LIST

A stream of prospective parents came to look round and to enter their sons, usually as babies. They were entered strictly in order and a waiting list was kept on the remote chance that someone on the firm list might cancel. The school has these entry books among its archives, handwritten by headmasters from the 1880s onwards. The constant review of the entry book is an unseen chore to which every headmaster has to devote time, running as fast as the red Queen to stay in the same place. Later headmasters looked back enviously on these postwar years as parents almost queued to see round the school.

Parents, often apprehensive on arrival, were given a comprehensive tour by the headmaster, meeting boys and staff en route and seeing whatever was going on. The boys regarded school visitors as their visitors and gladly showed them what they were doing. The tour was followed by a leisurely talk which often turned to girls' schools. One mother has entered Lambrook legend. In contrast with the hundreds of prospective parents who climbed upstairs to the dormitories and downstairs to the kitchens, who inspected lockers and loos, classrooms and changing rooms, wet fields and everything, this mother climbed only the front steps before flopping down in the drawing room saying to her husband "You go and look, dear: I'm sure it's all perfectly lovely!" The astonished headmaster did persuade her later to have a look at the nearer bits of his beloved school.

SMALL FORMS AND INDIVIDUAL ATTENTION

Archie was determined to keep the school as small as was viable so numbers crept up slowly: by 1950 there were 101 boys and the nine forms averaged 11 boys in each. Small forms and the best possible care for every individual with excellent teaching was what parents wanted.

Other schools had worse problems: George Chittenden was headmaster of a prep school in Seaford which closed in 1940 when the army commandeered its buildings. After the war, he called on Archie (they had earlier corresponded) saying he hoped to reopen his school. Now, whenever Archie had to disappoint parents, he suggested they go to Seaford where there was a fine man with a fine school which was reopening. So many of these parents liked what they saw that his school soon filled. George Chittenden asked Archie to take his son David as a young master when he was demobbed as he hoped David would one day succeed him in Seaford. Not only did David Chittenden learn schoolmastering at Lambrook but he married Mavis Montague Fuller, a delightful young assistant matron. They returned to Seaford in 1952 and their school grew into the Newlands Educational Trust, adapting to the changing needs of ensuing decades.

OUTINGS

Several marvellous opportunities came to the boys as restrictions eased. Lambrook had a double connection with Heathrow: a parent, Air Marshall Sir John d'Albiac, was Commandant of London Airport, and Sqdn. Leader J.R.Wardrop, an Old Boy, was Chief Administrative Officer of BOAC. They kindly invited 50 boys to come and look. In 1947 the airport was in its infancy as a civilian aerodrome and the Lambrook group was one of the first to be shown round. These visits were eagerly awaited and the

Chronicle records thanks to the instructors who "explained the Briefing and Meteorological sections so patiently" as well as thanks for inviting so many to tea, a considerable undertaking when rationing was still tight.

Later a Lambrook grandfather, Colonel Dyer, was in charge of the Royal Tournament and several times invited the whole school to the final dress rehearsal. These were wonderful outings, much enjoyed and endlessly discussed. The term logistics had not then been coined: suffice it to say that getting Lambrook to and from such an event was hard work when coach travel was a novelty but travel sickness was not.

MOVING TOWARDS PEACETIME

In June 1946 a marquee, still partly camouflaged after its wartime duties, was again erected close to the cricket field for the first Old Boys' Reunion, followed by Parents' Day a week later. Over a hundred Old Boys came to the Reunion and the crowded car park looked like peacetime again. A big Memorial Service was held in Chapel next day to commemorate the 80 Old Boys who died in World War 2.

The Chronicle, a skimpy leaflet for the past six years, returned to its prewar size though the dark green cover was still unobtainable. Even with shortages life began to feel more like peacetime, though not like pre war. Food rationing was still tight and bread was rationed for the first time this year. Clothes rationing continued and the work involved in the matrons' department was endless. Coping with clothes for growing children involved much making do and mending.

Domestically things remained difficult as few people actually chose to do cleaning work. Electric floor polishers and washing machines were still uncommon. Lambrook had daily helpers from the village – Mrs.Finch was invaluable in the sickrooms and dormitories for 29 years – but the era of foreign domestic workers began as schools needed resident staff for kitchen and dininghall. Best news of 1946 was the arrival of Dorothy Williams as assistant housekeeper for the next 36 years. Her tasks brought her in contact with everyone and she earned universal respect and affection.

THE ROYAL WEDDING IN NOVEMBER 1947

When Princess Elizabeth married Philip, Duke of Edinburgh, Lambrook celebrated with a whole holiday and the programme, to suit all tastes, included soccer seven a side matches followed by the broadcast service. Then the whole school and the staff put on fancy dress for lunch, followed by a siege in which the boys defended the school against a gang of unknown invaders. A special film show ended the day. The cartoon was enjoyed by all but one, who was escorted, howling, to the study. While the older boy rushed back to continue laughing, Archie asked the youngster what had made him so unhappy: "Oh Sir! They're doing such TERRIBLE things to Popeye!"

ANOTHER WEDDING

The first wedding in the Chapel had taken place in 1921 when Marjorie Browne, the headmaster's daughter, married Guy Cameron, an Old Boy on the staff. Now the second was planned in 1948, between the Reverend Philip Brownless and Isla Forbes. Anticipation by the boys was intense. One class began a confetti factory in May with a paper punch and a rota of boys to work it non stop till July! The marquee for Parents' Day was pitched at the top of the field by the Chapel this year and served for the wedding reception a few days later. Only the choir could squeeze into the Chapel for the service (one hopeful asked "Couldn't she have twelve singing pages?") but all the boys came to the reception, forming a guard of honour from the Chapel door. Very little confetti fell on the happy couple as the boys threw it all over the masters and matrons. Archie had asked Philip, then a curate in Southend on Sea, if he would like to be a schoolmaster but Philip had always intended to be a parish priest.

POSSIBLE SUCCESSORS AS HEADMASTER

By 1947 Archie was looking for a partner or a successor. The school was flourishing with a high reputation and a full entry book. The war had taken a heavy toll of Archie's health: now that Lambrook was clearly on the up and up, he wondered how long he could continue carrying a growing administrative burden which threatened to squeeze out his teaching and his time with the boys, the two reasons he became a schoolmaster in the first place.

The search for a partner proved fruitless. The nice ones had not enough capital and the rich ones were "just money grubbers". Archie felt he would betray the trust of present and future parents if he sold Lambrook to one of them. After two possible partners/successors had fallen through and he had dismissed thoughts of a dozen more, he decided to leave it for the time being.

This proved to be the lull before an astonishing storm.

AN INTERLUDE
STRANGER THAN FICTION: 1951

In 1949 there were three masters who shall be known here as Hook, Line and Sinker. Each had impeccable references which Archie Forbes had followed up as was his custom. When Hook and Line joined the staff, each said he wanted experience at Lambrook with its reputation as a training ground for headmasters but hoped later to run a school of his own. Now Archie asked Hook if he and his wife would like to run Lambrook as the senior partner, assisted by Line who was unmarried. They leapt at the idea of becoming joint headmasters. Sinker, wanting to put money into the school, became bursar and a junior partner. In May 1951, the Forbes family moved out of Lambrook to Brook Cottage, the Hook family moved into Lambrook, Line to Westfield and the Sinker family to Orchard House.

Phil Squarey, after 26 years at Lambrook teaching history and senior games, resigned in April and went to teach part time at Sunningdale. Archie kept out of Lambrook and flung himself into voluntary work for the Guide Dogs. To the amazement of the organisation, he raised over £11,000 in a year by writing personal letters to heads and pupils and by lecturing in schools all over the country. Busy as this kept him, he became aware that all was not well at Lambrook.

THE FIRST NEW HEADMASTER

At Christmas 1951, Line and Sinker told Hook they wanted to buy him out in April, the partnership not being all they had hoped. Line would become headmaster and Sinker would continue as bursar. If his partners had supported him, Hook might have been a good headmaster of Lambrook. Later he successfully ran a school elsewhere.

THE SECOND NEW HEADMASTER

In May 1952 when Line had been headmaster for a month, Brian Bentley, senior housemaster, called on Archie with evidence suggesting Line was not the upright man his references had described. The evidence was slight: how to get proof which would either exonerate Line or justify the suspicions? After grave discussion with Brian, Archie wrote a note to Line which Brian Bentley took back to school, inviting Line to call at Brook Cottage. When Line arrived, Archie said "I know what has been going on and I am shocked. I have asked you here so that you may tell me your side of the story. This is your opportunity to tell me everything." The bluff worked: people usually told Archie the truth. Line broke down and told him everything. He had kissed three boys: no, it had gone no further: yes, it had happened before, far in the past. He agreed to leave Lambrook at once but dreaded telling his mother. Archie suggested driving him over to his mother if Line would like him to explain it to her. Line agreed thankfully.

THE JUNIOR PARTNER

Then Archie, wondering how much Sinker knew, told Line that Sinker was owed an explanation for Line's imminent departure. Archie rang Sinker and invited him to Brook Cottage. Sinker came, whistling blithely. On seeing their faces, he stopped short and on hearing Line's confession he burst out "Oh, ******, you promised you wouldn't!" This damned Sinker in Archie's eyes as it revealed Sinker's earlier knowledge of Line.

Sinker returned across the field to his wife. They were now worried stiff about their money, invested in a school which was likely to fold up under this scandal. Sinker rang Archie begging him to become headmaster at once to prevent the immediate collapse of confidence in the school. While Flora kept Line at Brook Cottage with the whisky, Archie went to Lambrook to speak to Jim Rankin, senior master, and to ask for a suitcase of Line's things.

Christopher Eden, then a boy of 10, remembered Sinker "looking very flustered and red in the face" as he told the school that Mr. Line had left and Mr. Forbes was returning as headmaster. That night Archie drove the unhappy Line to his mother and had some hours' talk with them both.

THE OLD HEADMASTER AGAIN

Archie began a series of 20 hour days, leaving him as short of sleep as during the bombing. First, the staff had to be put in the picture. Second, Archie saw the 3 boys, explained matters and asked them please not to discuss it with other boys – he was available at any time. They were relieved to talk with him as they had been mystified by Line's "favouritism". Third, parental morale had taken a battering. Losing not one headmaster but two in six weeks suggested worse than carelessness! Archie told parents the whole story, writing and telephoning to the distant ones, speaking with nearer ones, who booked in at half hourly intervals until late at night. Soon word got round that he had the situation under control. The school's morale had sunk abysmally in 2½ terms so everyone had to be made to feel proud of themselves and the place. The last straw (the Forbes family only hoped it was the last) was discovering that in 2½ terms the trio had overspent and Lambrook was in the red for the first time ever.

However it was not the last straw: during June, Sinker became mentally unstable. It began with his inviting people to see what God had written on the blackboard in Form II. (This garish revelation was swiftly erased.) The doctor on several visits tried persuading Sinker to go voluntarily into hospital. When his wife awoke one night to find him standing over her with the carving knife the situation took on new urgency and off he went. It then transpired that this was not his first mental breakdown and that his brother in law (headmaster of a prominent public school) had been economical with the truth in assuring Archie of Sinker's robust health. Archie ended a 21 hour day calming Mrs. Sinker's financial fears. The money was complicated: Line and Sinker had together bought out Hook in April but already Mrs. Sinker needed her capital as it was doubtful if her husband would ever work again. Archie promised she should have it as soon as possible.

Unfortunately there is no record of what the boys wrote home. Their letters would probably have been on the lines of Ronald Searle's cartoon of a school in flames and a villainous headmaster creeping off with a glamourous little nurse while the boy laboriously writes "Nothing much has happened this week."

1950 AT JUNE SQUAREY'S WEDDING RECEPTION

1. R.A. Challenor
2. D.M.A. Powell
3. John D. Keeler
4. R.P.W. Millar
5. A.J.H. Saunders
6. W.G. Fiske
7. Peter K.W. Cashell
8. Martin H.T. Gairdner
9. John G. Nicholson
10. Brian H. Renwick
11. C.P. Lee
12. F.J. Irvine
13. W.G. Fischer
14. R.D.A. MacGregor
15. Moray J.C. Clouston
16. Charles L. Gimblett
17. Simon E. Hughes
18. Thomas V. Williams
19. R. John Bevan
20. Sandy Millar

21. J. Roger J. Stevens
22. Joscelyne P. Grove
23. Martin J.G. Cox
24. H.J. David Chads
25. R.P. Glyn Hughes
26. John P. Irving
27. Robin K. Sturdy
28. Christopher H, Hildesley
29. Michael F. Burdett
30. David J. FitzGerald

31. Colin J.K. Cunningham
32 John G. Murray
33. David S. Nairn
34. Colin Lindsay-MacDougall
35. I. Stuart Lyon
36. Richard J, Hildesley
37. Robin J.H. Payne
38. Nicholas G.A. Payne
39. Nicholas St.J.W.R. Lane
40. Christopher R.M. Eden

CHRISTOPHER EDEN

left Lambrook in 1953 and has spent most of his life Down Under. In 1996 he paid his first visit as an Old Boy and recognised everyone in this photograph without hesitation.

A.H.FORBES 1952-1956

Archie arranged to buy back the school though it was uncertain if he was buying a school or a white elephant. Legal advisors and accountants told him that Line, whose actions had almost closed Lambrook, would have no case in law if his money was not repaid in full. Archie replied that Line's money was dirty money and he intended repaying it in full, though Line must wait as Mrs Sinker needed hers at once.

Archie had an immense task. First Mrs.Sinker's share was repaid and Lambrook had to be pulled out of the red. Then began the years of instalment payments to Line. Badly needing a holiday, Archie and Flora booked a week in the Isle of Wight in August 1952 but cancelled for a sad reason. Rona, their younger daughter, flew back from Nigeria with her desperately ill baby, Robert, who died in Great Ormond Street Hospital a week later. Flora stayed in London with Rona while Archie walked the dogs locally yet again saying his heart hadn't been fixed on that holiday anyway: he would rather see something of Rona on this short sad visit.

CHANGES IN THE MASTERS' COMMON ROOM

The departures of Hook, Line and Sinker were followed by two unexpected sorrows. Mr Morley Brown, appointed to teach history in 1951, died in 1952. Then the young Norman Bazell, appointed in 1952 to take games, boxing and middle maths, died suddenly in 1953, leaving his widow with a little girl of 5 and a baby boy of four months. These last blows really shook the community which was working hard to recreate the stability of only two years before.

James Allcock arrived to take top English, Bryan Jones to do geography and senior games, and in 1953 came Robert Sopwith, senior classicist. His previous headmaster almost shed tears at losing him because they could not provide married accommodation. He stayed for 15 years, one of the trio of masters referred to by younger colleagues as "The Druids"

THE CORONATION

Meanwhile King George VI had died in February 1952 and the country was planning for the Coronation of Queen Elizabeth in June 1953. Lambrook had a four day recess. Archie wrote "Boys disappeared to all parts of the country and returned with wonderful accounts of their experiences. A few braved the weather all night to get a good view of the procession and even the half dozen who stayed here saw Lambrook under such changed conditions that they will not forget either the Coronation or the recess for many long years." He would not forget "taking them to see the decorations in London and being jammed for an hour in the traffic of Trafalgar Square after which the car boiled in the Haymarket where the boys fervently hoped they would remain for the rest of the night!" This little group were invited by Dean of Windsor to the special Coronation Service in St. George's Chapel, Windsor.

LOOKING AHEAD

Through all these events, local and national, the family wondered how long Archie could continue working so hard and whether talk of a successor would make the parents nervous. It certainly made the family nervous! By 1953 Philip Brownless had served 7 years in Southend, first as a curate and latterly as priest in charge of a huge parish. He wrote to his bishop and to his first vicar about his next step, enquiring what they thought about his becoming a schoolmaster if opportunity presented. He expected them both to say a firm no – that he should remain a parish priest. To his surprise both gave unequivocal support to the idea. Archie was overjoyed. It solved the problem of the succession as the Brownless family were already known to many parents and to the staff.

ARCHIE AND FLORA FORBES
in 1952.

In April 1954 Philip and Isla Brownless moved to Orchard House with Alison aged 4 and Andrew aged 2. Philip became chaplain and flung himself into teaching scripture, history, rugger and swimming. He was to learn his trade and get to know everyone before becoming first a partner and later headmaster. The school was going well with a fine staff, superb academic and athletic achievements and boys of every ability thriving. Money was tight as the old buildings ate it up and Line was still being paid off.

Rona and Raymond Hunter came back from Nigeria to live at Brook Cottage in 1955 and their new baby, Charles, was born in November. Raymond became Lambrook's bursar, lifting much work and worry from Archie's shoulders.

BEGINNING TO SEE FINANCIAL DAYLIGHT

In 1956 the last payment went to Line. Archie's relief was indescribable. He and Flora began talking about a fishing holiday, their first since 1938. A new car became a possibility at last.

The summer term went swimmingly but as everyone dispersed for the holidays, Archie turned yellow with jaundice. An exploratory operation in August revealed an inoperable cancer. Flora was told he might live six months but three months was more likely.

While ill, Archie prepared three timetables for September, one if he was back in harness, another if he could work part time, and a third without him. His last energy was spent smoothing the way ahead. The family aimed to keep things as normal as possible for the boys, and the prognosis was only known to the family and to the school nurse, Phyllis Goldwin, an old friend. When the autumn term began, Archie enjoyed visitors, either in his bedroom or at the car window if Flora drove him round to the playground.

On his bedroom door hung a reversible notice saying "Please don't disturb" or "Visitors welcome". One day Flora came upstairs, surprised by the volume of happy chat from his room, to find 35 boys had squeezed in to talk to him. On seeing the "Visitors welcome" sign one boy had run to fetch the others quickly. Few knew how near death he was. He died on 31 October, aged 57.

A fortnight earlier Philip Brownless told the boys that Ben had been born at Orchard House and, in accordance with tradition, they would have a half holiday later in the term. Now he broke the news of Archie's death. Since this news was a greater shock for others than for the family, Flora took care to soften it for the boys. A Thanksgiving service in Winkfield Church was fixed for November 5 th, the private funeral having taken place earlier. The Rev.John Eddison gave the address at the big service. Archie had modelled his sermons on those of John Eddison whom he regarded as the outstanding preacher to prep schools. It was an inspiring service with full throated singing from the school, the village, parents and Old Boys.

Some people expected the fireworks and bonfire to be postponed but Flora intended the service to be followed by this eagerly awaited evening. Archie was the last person to think it improper for the school to sing beautifully at his service in the afternoon and finish the evening marching round the bonfire, singing "Ten green bottles" with their mouths full of toffee. The family was determined that school life should go on smoothly and it did, but at considerable personal cost, especially to Flora. She worked untiringly for Lambrook and for her two families of grandchildren for a further 35 years.

A DIGRESSION ON READING ALOUD

IN THE DAYS BEFORE TV AND RADIO, to have a story read aloud was a treat. Mrs. Browne's Sunday reading was "an amazing innovation" in 1904 according to C.L.Norris Elye. On Sunday evenings, with their handful of sweets (called "shop") boys sprawled on the drawing room floor for the next instalment of a book read by a member of staff, often the headmaster or his wife. From 1910 onwards A.E.Fernie read to the senior boys and Mrs. Browne to the juniors. Her favourite book was about a highwayman, *Nutbrown Roger and I*. Fifty years later, S.K. Rutherford recalled the pleasure of hearing Archie Forbes read *It's Never Too Late To Mend* and *Robbery Under Arms*, adding "Bless all those dear folk who helped to make our youth happy."

Some books seem to be acceptable to all generations but once a book is dramatised on TV the surprise element is lost and it cannot be read aloud for five years or so. *Moonfleet* by Meade Faulkner was a case in point. Archie read this at regular intervals throughout four decades as well as *The Riddle of the Sands* by Erskine Childers and most of John Buchan. A fast moving story is essential.

Dornford Yates, Masefield's *John Davis* and E.F. Benson's *The Luck of the Vails* were all popular with the senior reading in the '20s and '30s. As the school grew, it was divided into three for Sunday reading and Flora's middle school group widened in age range. Choosing a book to read aloud to 60 boys is difficult. Gerald Durrell and Hammond Innes went down well in the '70s.

Choosing a book to read to the whole school in more difficult still but both Guy and Archie used sometimes to read aloud for the last 10 minutes of boys' tea. Mr. Browne read *A Cricketo-Detective Story* by C.A.Alington. The boys' entries in the Story Competition were read in tea and were enjoyed partly because they were funny and also because the authors' anonymity was transparent. The domestic staff, especially the Portuguese in the '60s with limited English, leaned through the hatch and loved them too. The Prize Story was not read as it was printed in *The Chronicle*.

Boys in the sickroom were read to regularly. Reading a story in one sickroom is a pleasant task. Flora remembered a trickier assignment when she

---

Flora Forbes read to boys for more than half a century. She learned the tricks of the trade from Archie:

1 *Remove it from the school library so no one can read it quickly and spill the beans half way through.*

2 *Read the book carefully beforehand and mark the cuts so they are undetectable.*

3 *If anyone gets fidgety, don't read louder, read more quietly – his neighbours will soon make him sit still.*

sat in the top corridor with a torch reading to five or six dormitories simultaneously. The boys were being nursed in semi darkness in the big measles epidemic of 1938.

In World War 2, Archie read by torchlight to the whole school on their bunks and palliasses in the basement during air raids. It diverted attention away from the regular 'crump' of bombs or guns and made a peaceful atmosphere in which even the fearful could drop off to sleep.

A group entitled to a special story were the choir before the Carol Service when it was held in Winkfield Church. They had to sit still and keep quiet in their clean surplices in a small space at the back of the church while the congregation assembled. Finding a suitably gripping story to read in a whisper and lasting exactly 25 minutes was a taxing task for a matron.

R.V.Johns read to the junior boys for more than 20 years but lately matrons have read to the juniors upstairs on Sundays. Nowadays TV and video, although rationed, have eroded the time available and being read to is no longer the regular pleasure of former days.

THE REV. PHILIP BROWNLESS

6

THE REV. P. P. S. BROWNLESS
HEADMASTER
1956–1971

MONEY MATTERS AND MECHANISATION

WHAT WAS THIS NEW HEADMASTER LIKE? How long would he last ? Philip Brownless was 35, a clergyman, a historian and an energetic rugger player. He had been at Lambrook for two years. Time would tell, said the sages, but there was not much time.

When headmasters of prep schools change, everyone feels nervous and this was well justified when schools were privately owned. Parents' perceptions of success or failure could soon result in the demise of a school. The new man must quickly make his mark with staff, boys, parents AND the bank manager: he must appraise the school's past strengths and weaknesses, and assess its future with regard to the national scene politically, economically and socially. He must get to know everybody quickly and have time for each one.

Faced with this job description we, for this chapter is written in the first person, marvel at how swiftly headmasters fit in, quietly moulding schools to their new directions. It is greatly to the credit of recent headmaster couples at Lambrook that they have succeeded without the advantage Philip had in 1956 of already knowing the staff, boys and parents. Thankfully, no headmaster since then has started with the financial burden which became evident when Archie died.

His last year was a triumphant one for Lambrook: academically, athletically and pastorally the school was second to none with a staff other schools envied. Parental confidence, that fragile plant, had revived. Though the public face of Lambrook looked good, Archie had only just finished paying off Line. The school was a Limited Company and the shares were now in Archie's name. He and Flora had no funds outside Lambrook. Financial arrangements for the future were at an early stage when his cancer intervened.

DEATH DUTIES

In 1956 a widow had to pay inheritance tax on her husband's estate. This law was changed a few years later. The Limited Company thus became liable for colossal death duties and the sole source of funds was the school fees. The enormity of this liability was a millstone round the family's neck. Continuing Lambrook as Archie would have wished became a kind of war to prevent its bankruptcy. Not a word of this could be mentioned to a soul. The sorrow of friends and colleagues was unifying and the staff pulled together wonderfully. Senior masters knew Philip was inexperienced as a schoolmaster but the debacle of five years earlier was fresh in their minds. What they did not know was how close loomed financial disaster nor how skilled a businessman he would prove to be. Without the financial acumen and prudent management of Philip and Derek Don, of whom more shortly, Lambrook would have gone under.

Two other old friends of Lambrook died within those few weeks as well. One was Guy Cameron, lifelong friend and headmaster with Archie in the 1930s, and the second was Ted Coxhead, who spent 42 years at Lambrook, first as gardener's boy and since 1921 as Head Gardener with responsibility for the whole estate. His death made urgent the reorganising of the archaic heating systems and the care of the grounds.

During Archie's financial transactions with Hook, Line and Sinker, he had been much impressed with their young accountant, Derek Don, who likewise admired Archie. In 1956 with Lambrook facing financial ruin, Philip asked Derek Don for advice. His office in London was sparsely furnished with a desk bare of all clutter. On the wall hung the text "In all thy ways acknowledge Him and He will direct thy paths." Derek Don was a wise friend to both generations of the family. When he began specialising in school accountancy he was highly valued elsewhere too.

Derek Don's advice was prompt and detailed: he briefed Philip on how to show round the tax inspector who was due to assess the value of Lambrook, even the oak trees, so as to put an exact figure on the 'widow's liability'. All this happened within a couple of weeks of Archie's death, while the school continued busily. 115 boys and a baby a month old all needed feeding frequently.

Philip put a freeze on all expenditure but this was known only to the family who had earnest discussions in the study. Budgets were monitored, wartime habits of making do and mending continued. Archie had not drawn a regular salary and Philip felt Lambrook could only afford to pay him his assistant master's salary, rather less than most of the other masters.

In December 1956 the Brownless family moved into Lambrook and Flora Forbes moved to Orchard House where she looked after 18 boys at night, supervising the workroom and young matrons in Lambrook by day. There had not been a baby in Lambrook for half a century when the domestic scene was utterly different. To make possible some family privacy, the former handicraft room beneath the drawing room became the Brownless family room, named Very Down because it was the lowest floor. A doorway was knocked through to give access to the back stairs which led up (and up and up) past the study door to the bedrooms above. Very Down was a lifesaver: the family could be silly or sad or noisily cheerful away from the public gaze. Rightly has the existence of a headmaster's family in the middle of a boarding school been called the goldfish bowl.

It was important, though, that boys should feel we were readily available. One new boy discovered the way to Very Down and turned up several times after school breakfast. I was spooning mush into the baby's mouth and this 8 year old looked at him with considerable disfavour. "I just came to see what you were doing" he said and departed happily after a brief conversation. Next day he came again and told me what his mother would be doing at that time of day. He liked to know what everyone was up to. It can be a valuable trait: some years later he became a governor of Lambrook.

MECHANISATION AND MODERNISATION

Two areas, mowing and stoking, needed urgent attention. Before the war, four men had worked under Ted Coxhead, looking after the grounds and stoking seven coke fired boilers four times daily. Some of the boilers Ted had nursed were due for retirement as was the 30 inch Dennis which had mown the cricket field for twenty years. Now the mowing had increased to 13 acres, a tractor and triple gang mower were needed. By degrees oil fired boilers were installed in Lambrook, Westfield and Orchard House and to heat the swimming bath. Raymond Hunter, Lambrook's first bursar, had two men to look after it all. In addition he did the school accounts, saw contractors, supervised buildings and repairs and turned his own skilful hand to whichever job was most urgent. His land drainage scheme created two new playing fields. When he and Rona went full time into farming, first at Maidens Green in 1958 and later in Dorset, they were much missed. Words cannot convey the anxiety, the conundrums, the ifs and buts which family conferences had to resolve, remembering that Lambrook was primarily a school.

The Easter holidays were always busy with little time to turn the golf course and rugger pitches into cricket fields. The outside was run as a smallholding with a few Hereford cattle and some pigs in the Westfield styes. A huge sow escaped one day and galloped into the middle of a cricket match, pursued by Jim O'Leary on a bicycle calling "Come on, me daarlint". They did a lap of honour to laughter and applause before she trotted away after his kindly clucking voice.

Philip visited the bank manager with a business plan and returned with an overdraft arrangement. The school balance fluctuated predictably, high tide at the start of term and low tide at the end when salaries were paid, with a very low ebb every August. The overdraft facility provided flexibility as the bank would not worry if the school account dipped briefly into the red during the holidays. This flexibility was used, amongst other things, for investing money at the start of each term at a time in the '60s when the wily investor could make money. Thus was capital produced for tractors, boilers and buildings.

Derek Don and Philip also initiated a block fee scheme which suited a few parents. Lambrook was probably the first prep school to run their own scheme and the rates compared favourably with those of public schools offering such schemes. Five years' fees in a lump was a welcome injection of capital: one boy was gratefully known behind the scenes as 'the boiler boy'. A new headmaster dare not raise the fees and Lambrook's connection was not wealthy: we knew many parents were tightening their family belts to afford the fees. They must not know how tight was Lambrook's belt.

When the bank manager again asked to see Philip as head office were looking into overdraft facilities, it sounded ominously as though they might withdraw the arrangement which had proved so helpful. He set off apprehensively but returned smiling with the overdraft facility doubled!

Charitable status was now under consideration as an appropriate way of ensuring the school's future. Points in favour were that moneys given in a future appeal would be free of tax, death duties would not be payable provided Flora lived another seven years (she was just 60 and insured herself against dying too soon), and the headmaster would enjoy the support of a governing body. But, and it seemed a big BUT to Flora, the concept of ownership must disappear: she felt this was giving away Archie's life work. Derek Don's judicious advice was invaluable. When all were agreed and Lambrook became a Charitable Trust in 1967, Derek Don was the first person the family asked to become a Governor.

> *First things first.*
> *At this time a conversation at home was reported back to us;-*
> *Brother of 7, not yet at Lambrook:*
>   *"Mr.Brownless must be awfully rich if the parents all*
>   *pay him so much money."*
> *Brother of 9, already at Lambrook:*
>   *"No, he isn't at all rich really. He has to spend*
>   *most of it on food."*

THE CHAPEL EXTENSION IN 1959

Old Boys, shocked by the deaths in quick succession of Archie and Guy, asked what form a memorial to these two should take. The Chapel was now the tight spot into which 113 boys squeezed uncomfortably. Lambrook had never had an appeal but now the money rolled in and plans were made to extend the Chapel by pushing out the west wall and adding a gallery. E.C. Hughes of Wokingham did the work beautifully in spite of bad weather and in February 1959 it was dedicated by the Bishop of Reading. It was wonderful to have room for visitors while retaining the intimacy of a school Chapel.

A staircase was built in 1959 to the attics above the classrooms, giving space for a nature room and a new IVA where senior boys felt grandly elevated above the *hoi polloi*. Soon the need for specialist classrooms became pressing. Brian Bentley had long carried around a tape recorder, electric leads and adaptors as well as a heap of French books. Science was assuming greater importance and a proper laboratory and storeroom were needed. In 1967 the roof of the old classroom block was removed to add a new floor for a lab and storeroom, a History/Geography room and a French room where Brian installed his audio visual aids and hung posters of chateaux and cheeses. It presented a chic contrast to the classrooms of former years.

When E.C. Hughes had extended the Chapel, the boys' friendly interest had impressed the workmen and the managing director who entered his two sons. At last the school had obtained planning permission to build on the site of a derelict cottage fronting Winkfield Row, so E.C. Hughes built this first house and the Bentley family moved in 1962 when Brian ceased being housemaster to the 50 senior boys sleeping in Westfield. The converted kennels, invaluable in the housing shortage 20 years earlier, were no longer comfortable dwellings. A thunderstorm and a blocked land drain caused a flood which made instant refugees of their inhabitants so brick bungalows were built in 1968. The Strong Brothers of Reading generously erected all three for little more than the cost of two. Planning permission was granted if these houses shared Westfield's access to the road.

OLD BOYS

Visits from Old Boys were frequent and enjoyed by staff and boys. Between 40 and 50 boys, a third of the school, had Old Boy fathers or uncles. Parents' Day was in effect an Old Boys' Day and dozens of young Old Boys came back from their public schools on the last Saturday in June to meet each other and to reminisce with staff over whom they now towered. We thus had a good idea what was happening in the public schools. This strong connection with the past was a legacy from Archie: we wondered if it would remain as strong under a new regime.

Three Old Boys came to visit Lambrook in 1959 for the first time since they had left in 1900. Philip had two pairs of prospective parents to show round that Saturday and asked me to tour with the past as he was busy with the future. We should all meet at teatime in the drawing room. His first couple came at 2 pm and ended with tea: his next pair were due for tea at 4 pm and would tour with him afterwards. Thank goodness Mrs.Simpson, a marvellous 80 year old who came twice a week to serve drawing room tea, would be on duty: I could therefore enjoy guests, knowing that Mrs.Simpson would take phone calls and welcome any unexpected visitors.

My trio, three of the five Gray brothers at Lambrook between 1890 and

1900, were delightful and I saw Victorian Lambrook through their eyes. They began by ushering me politely through doorways but were soon so excited I panted in their wake as they flung open doors, even Sister's bedroom which they had expected to be a sickroom. They snorted at soft modernisations like the bathroom with six baths – they had one bath a week when a maid combed their hair with a steel comb – and on reaching the Maltese Cross, their dormitory on the top floor, they rushed to the farthest bed and fell on their knees to peer into the corner. Six eyes turned accusingly on me: "YOU HAVE LAID DOWN LIN - O - LE - UM !" Dormitory rivalry was intense in their day and 'sacrifices' were made by dropping a valued object between the floorboards before an important occasion. Since the linoleum was older than me, I did not feel guilty about it. I begged Audley Gray to write down their marvellous reminiscences and later he sent *Lambrook in 1900* from which I have gratefully drawn in earlier chapters. The only person who did not enjoy their enthusiasm was a two year old prospective Lambrookian, horrified when three old men in turn shook his hand from a very great height.

POLITICS AGAIN

The 1950s produced another threat to the prep schools but from a surprising source, the public schools! Led by the Headmaster of Eton, Robert Birley, they tried to persuade the state to fund places at public schools so they could take the cream of the state system as assisted bursars. They wanted the prep schools to have these boys between the ages of 11 and 13 to prepare them for public schools and cram them for Common Entrance. Philip, very new at a meeting of Incorporated Association of Preparatory Schools headmasters, was buttonholed by a public school headmaster, one of 'Birley's boys', lobbying for the scheme. After hearing his spiel, Philip said if such a crackpot scheme came into being he would go straight back to being a parish priest: big surprise! The prep schools were angered by this proposal which felt like a stab in the back. It undercut their purpose, which was all round education, reducing them to cramming French and Latin into the unfortunate state bursars who were, it seemed, to be regarded simply as fodder for the public schools. The Labour government of the time made it clear to the public schools that the scheme was a non starter.

Ironically, it was not long afterwards that a group of public school headmasters, meeting informally, discovered they were going to be short of entries a term or two ahead. They at once began wining and dining prep school headmasters! Life then settled into a routine of healthy competition to the great benefit of both sides. The preparatory schools, who were now taking science seriously, benefited from this greater cooperation. The Malvern Science Course offered a useful syllabus for prep schools. It was sponsored by Shell who loaned kits of equipment to selected schools.

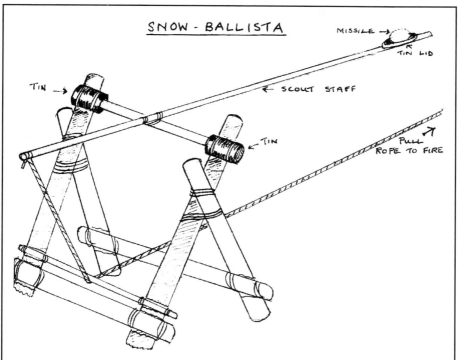

SNOW - BALLISTA

ALL ROPES AND LASHINGS ARE SHOWN IN RED INK

TROOP MEETING THURSDAY 8th OCT 1430 HOURS

1. The Troop (less those receiving knotting instruction from Mr Footner) will construct one or more of the above weapons during Thursday afternoon.

2. PLs and QMs should RV in the Troop Stores on Wednesday next between 1600 and 1730 hrs to select stores. The SM will be present to give advice, if required.

3. All PLs should copy the above plan, unless they are able to commit all details to memory.

4. If snow has NOT fallen by next Thursday, it will be necessary to improvise some other form of missile. In view of the fact that the General Election is taking place on that day, a mud pie may be appropriate.

5. NO SHOT may be fired UNLESS THE SM IS PRESENT.

C. G. Eastange
S.M. Lambrook Troop

5 Oct 54

THE SIXTIES

The Sixties have come to be seen as a time of license, of freedom 'busting out all over', of teenagers flush with money, of drugs, of shacking up. Previously dependable words developed new meanings, gay, rave, partner, square, as did new combinations like student power, youth culture and sit in. What delighted the young and shook their elders was that – suddenly it seemed - life in all its fullness was available for the taking. The boast of an early credit card – that it 'took the waiting out of wanting' – seemed to be coming true. Rumours of rebellion and strikes, even invasion by rent-a-mob aliens, were heard from universities and schools, though Frank Fisher replied to a query about Wellington that he had "nothing worse to deal with than schoolboy pranks, sensible, straightforward and unsordid."

How did Lambrook fare under this social revolution? Changes occurred slowly: of course some boys were impatient – "Why can't we wear home clothes at weekends?" – but after discussing even such a simple proposition they seemed content with the status quo. Progress seemed to them snail paced. Younger boys, sticklers for tradition, greeted even a small change with "Oh! but Sir, we've ALWAYS done it the other way!" while older boys teased Philip with "Oh Sir, you are so square, Sir!" Mostly we were all too busy with our own activities to do more than gape at the speed of change outside.

On the first day of term, it was Philip's custom to ask boys what they had been doing in the holidays, who had been fishing, who had been abroad, who had made anything interesting etc. Once he asked if anyone had broken the law during the holidays. Instead of the awkward silence he half expected, this was greeted with a titter of amusement as about half the school put their hands up! Most of the offences concerned smuggling or under age driving (on private property). Another "hands up" revealed that 11 boys had fallen fully dressed into deep water during the summer holidays, thus emphasising the importance of swimming lessons. Apparently X deserved his ducking by standing up in a canoe but Y, on a dockside, had stepped on a fish and slipped into deep and dirty water. Applause!

HARD WORK IN CLASS

Hard work was what boys had come to Lambrook for and in retrospect it is surprising that so much else was fitted into each 24 hours. The secret lay partly in boarding - no time spent on daily journeys – but mainly in versatile staff who devoted energy and high expectations to golf, fives, chess, Punch and Judy, play writing and performance, public speaking, scouting, camping, gardening and much else. The postwar baby boomers who were now in their early teens, found the public schools picking and choosing among the press of candidates.

NO ENTRY TEST

Lambrook had no entry test for new boys. Most were entered as babies or toddlers and were taken in order of booking. Those on the waiting list hoped someone on the firm list would fall out but this was rare. Boys came at 8½, some from private schools and some from state primary schools of widely varying standards. This was the era of the hated 11 Plus selection for secondary education and parents had two fears: would their financial plans cope with the fees at both prep and public school and would their son do well enough in Common Entrance. If frustrated by either obstacle he would not only have little choice of secondary school but would be joining a different system two years later than his peers. Some financially apprehensive parents asked that their sons should take the 11 Plus as a precaution.

The 1962 *Chronicle* gave some figures in response to these concerns. "Since 1955, 29 boys have taken the 11 Plus: 18 qualified for grammar school education and 11 did not. Of the 18, five gained scholarships to public schools and another five are likely scholars, so the boys who have taken this examination are an above average sample of Lambrook boys and it would be true to say that if the whole school were to take the 11 Plus, quite 50% would fail. Now what of the 11 who failed? All secured places at public schools, all who have reached the age of 16 have done five or more O levels and the handful who are old enough have taken or are taking A levels. Under the state system it would have been regarded as very creditable if any of them had secured one or two O levels."

SOME LOW READING AGES

Of 112 boys leaving between 1957 and 1962, 5 boys (4.5%) had failed to get into a public school, and all five had reading ages much below their real ages: one eight year old and three nine year olds could barely read on arrival and one English boy of 10½ who had lived abroad was unable to read a single word in any language!

The 1963 *Chronicle* spelled out what a boy should know on arriving at Lambrook: " to read reasonably fluently, to be able to write and to know his multiplication tables up to 12 times. While many boys fulfil these requirements and have gone beyond them, it is alarming the number who do not. Boys still arrive unable to read properly, with primitive ideas of making any letters at all, and unable to say more than their 2 or 3 times table. This means that two crucial years of a boy's education have been wasted and he is likely to have to pay the price of this right the way through his schooling. Parents ought to take a hand in dealing with this problem, partly by insisting that children are taught the necessary elements at the schools they attend, i.e. down with the 'don't believe in making children learn tables by heart' brigade, and partly by some unobtrusive help at home. Sending a boy to a preparatory school in good time will not make good a lack earlier."

The fact that these untaught boys, and others who were not academic, seemed to thrive and enjoy Lambrook is perhaps the greatest tribute to the staff. The atmosphere was one in which everyone was valued and expected to contribute to the whole. It was a pleasure to watch a boy, who was academically slow but with music in his feet, kindly and slowly demonstrating a Scottish dance step to his partner, a budding scholar.

BRIGHT BOYS

None of the awards and later successes of the bright boys came without hard work. One, later a top scholar, used to read ahead in his textbook and masters sometimes tried to catch him with a question on what the class were actually learning. He got it right every time though half his mind was several pages ahead.

Another won an Eton Scholarship and his delighted parents suggested he could take the rest of the term easily. His reply surprised them: "That's not how we do it at Lambrook: it's after the scholarship is over that the masters really see what we can do: that's how they become good teachers." Certainly the work done after exams became a challenge of its own. Jim Rankin taught code breaking, ciphers and the like. Brian Bentley sometimes branched into German and taught about cars and engines in French. Several boys took French, Latin and Greek O levels on arrival at their public schools. Guy Baird's Wellington timetable was so full he dropped Greek but he freewheeled through O level a year after his last lesson with Robert Sopwith. Of the 358 pupils who left in those fifteen years, 17.5% won scholarships and 14 of the 63 scholarships were top ones, including Charterhouse (twice) Cheltenham, Harrow, Marlborough (3 times), Radley, Rugby, Sherborne (twice), Wellington (twice) and Wycombe Abbey.

One father, on returning from abroad and wondering how to choose a prep school with first class teaching, studied lists of public schools' scholarships while commuting in the train. He wanted to learn which preparatory school won a regular stream of scholarships and – more importantly – to a wide variety of good schools. Lambrook came out top so he brought his wife to look round and make sure the care of the boys matched up to the teaching.

He, like others before him, was surprised that potential scholars had no special coaching, no extra half hours at bedtime or in break, that no workbooks were allowed in dormitories, that the standards were achieved because the teaching throughout the school was of the same calibre. Often good CE candidates, placed in scholars' forms at their public schools, ended their first year ahead of scholars from elsewhere.

HALF TERM EXEAT

A half term exeat of two nights was introduced tentatively in 1964 and soon became a fixture. As cars and roads improved and quarantines were discarded, parents visited three or four times a term and schools welcomed greater parental involvement. The double journey for a day visit home imposed a strain on drivers and passengers. The exeat solved this at once, was pronounced a success and soon grew to 3 nights. the school did not close: anyone remaining was looked after and entertained.

MASTERS AND HOWLERS

NAME	YEARS AT LAMBROOK		SUBJECTS / ACTIVITIES
J.M.Rankin	1935-1972	37	Maths, top games, Scouts, fives, chess.
J.B.Bentley	1937-1981	44	French, soccer, films, golf, Housemaster
R.V.Johns	1944-1967	23	Junior forms, cricket, soccer, gardens
R.Sopwith	1953-1968	15	Classics, soccer, junior games
D.G.Backhouse	1956-1967	11	Junior maths, top cricket & rugger
G.G.Footner	1958-1993	34	Maths, Housemaster, swimming, carpentry
N.W.Nicholson	1958-1965	7	English, soccer, tennis
C.G.Eastaugh	1959-1982	23	English, Scouts, Housemaster
C.G.Ward	1962-1982	20	Geography, middle Latin, all games
R.R.Johnson	1967-1994	27	Science, fives, Housemaster, windband
E.L.Horsfall	1968-1981	13	Top games, junior forms

These remarkable masters were the backbone of the staff for half a century, showing young masters how it was done and teaching two generations of many families. Their skill, loyalty and willingness were unstinted. The stately trio of Jim Rankin, Brian Bentley and Robert Sopwith, ancient to eight year olds, were highly regarded throughout the prep school world. Irreverent colleagues referred to them as The Druids. They, with R.V. Johns, were already in post when the new headmaster took on in 1956. Young blood was needed to complement the skills of this older generation. Enter several who could have held top posts elsewhere. Lambrook gained greatly in having men of such calibre teaching the middle and lower school. They were all interesting people even after long years of teaching in the same school! Small wonder those boys were well grounded.

The female of hero is heresy

Jim Rankin was an able mathematician and an all rounder. His lessons stretched the boys' minds. In the '60s the Schools Mathematical Project (New Maths) was being tried in a number of schools. He incorporated the best of the old with the new and his modifications were soon adopted elsewhere. He oversaw the timing and manner in which Nuffield Science was introduced and later still prepared the way for computer science to become part of the curriculum. He was a skilled coach who had run all three top games and the Scouts with great precision. With staves and cord lashings the boys built elegant bridges across the stream which were tried out by visitors of all sizes. At one camp there were eight fires with biscuit tin ovens for the Sunday roast, with Yorkshire pudding, roast potatoes, greens and gravy. The Scoutmaster carved and there was a special oven to keep his helping hot until everyone else had been served. He coached fives in free time to an amazing standard. Both Patrick Cashell at Westminster and Richard Keeler at Lancing captained their schools, Michael Macray won a half blue at Oxford and Michael Elliott captained Oxford and with his partner won the All England Doubles in 1962. Twenty five years later Dr.Michael Elliott gave much of his spare time to coaching another generation of Lambrook fives players. Jim Rankin could see behind him while writing on the blackboard and would reprimand a malefactor without turning round.

JIM RANKIN
with, (on his right) Peter Greene and, (on his left) Michael Hildesley

BRIAN BENTLEY
and his new French room.

Nelson was killed by a snipper.

Brian Bentley was universally admired. He had a fine tenor voice and his lessons were fun. Boys had to work hard but they wanted to do well for him. He taught French as a living language long before this was called the 'New French'. The 1954 inspectors thought him outstanding and gave him a six week refresher course at the University of Poitiers. One father proclaimed on the front steps "The fees are worth it for the French teaching alone!" When their car had broken down, ten year old son's fluency with French mechanics saved their holiday. Hundreds of boys learned their first golf strokes from him – he was a very good golfer – and he rolled those spongy greens with care. His talk to golfers at the start of a season included stern words about safety and about Words Heard On Other Golf Courses Which Are Not To Be Used At Lambrook. He was a wonderful housemaster, with the help of his wife Cora, first at Orchard House and later to 50 senior boys at Westfield. He was a mine of information about the film industry and the tastes of young viewers. His film shows are gratefully remembered, especially by pre TV generations.

Masters are like minefields: as soon as you do
something wrong, somebody blows up.

The third of the trio, **Robert Sopwith**, may have seemed a little fierce when first encountered in the classroom but he was skilled at making Latin and Greek interesting. Older boys valued his stimulating table talk. All the masters took pleasure in the later achievements of boys they had taught but in 1963 he had good reason to rejoice. Four young Old Boys, together in his top set five years earlier, won classical scholarships simultaneously, two to Oxford and two to Cambridge. He carried his umbrella in the on guard position as he walked briskly into school and it was a miracle that no boy running out to PT was impaled upon it. His standards of accuracy and application gradually rubbed off on his pupils.

The Tarpeian rock was meant to be a sracked stone
in Ireland which people go to and kiss.

R.V. Johns, a gentle, shy man, was the first master whom new boys got to know, easing the the early days of boarding school for many. He delighted in tricks and toys and and small mysteries such as the magnetic ladybird that walked across his lapel. Soon after term began, he would sidle up to the headmaster and tell him which of the new boys would be scholars in five years' time and he was nearly always right. He had been a county hockey player, a good club cricketer and much was owed to his coaching of junior games. One Under 11 team were sluggish batsmen until RVJ rashly offered a Mars Bar for every run over 50 which any batsman scored. Richard Sears promptly made 104! RVJ wrote so appealingly to the Mars factory in Slough that a parcel of Mars Bars arrived with a letter thanking RVJ for a fine advertisement and adding their congratulations to the 'Garfield Sobers of Winkfield Row'. He supervised the boys' gardens, pipe in mouth, and considered carefully before passing judgement on a weed or awarding damages as in the Case of the Stolen Strawberry. Anyone daunted at organising party games for a dozen nine year olds can only gasp at RVJ's stamina in exercising 60 youngsters on Sunday afternoons for years and years. They played games all over the grounds, often variants of 'French and English'. That was not the end of his Sunday though: he read a book to the 20 youngest boys while they sucked sweets in the hour between tea and bed. It was sadly true that he found the holidays too long. After retiring, he stayed on to run the stationery cupboard and the boys' gardens.

Q. *What do you know about the Duke of Wellington ?*
A. *It's the pub wot we buy our beer at.*

George Footner had an old fashioned courtesy which enabled him to absorb the best from older masters and produce his own new methodical teaching. Maths was his major contribution. It was valuable too that he preached in Chapel. He introduced computing when it became a timetable subject. For 23 years he and Susanna ran Orchard House, a serene haven for 18 middle school boys. The pleasure of Westfield and Orchard House boys at going across the grounds for a pleasant hour before bed was clear. When he was young, George was good at putting people of any age at their ease: when he was old he was even better at it.

Q. Give a prefix for the opposite of sense.
A. Incense.

Neville Nicholson, a wonderful games player with half blues for lawn tennis and squash looked after top English, the 1st game soccer and did wonders with the tennis. Under his guidance, Lambrook entered the Prep Schools Wimbledon for the second time in 1960 and his pupils did well: the first couple, Vane and Surtees, were runners up in the doubles finals.

Walpole was a wig who kept himself in power
with offers of royal paternity.

Neville Nicholson and Colin Eastaugh, an engaging and persuasive team, fostered the boys' interest in English which had less classroom time than it merited for its importance in later life. The English folders had the same aim. It was an honour for a boy to be invited to provide a fair copy of some work for the current English folder in the library. Occasionally a boy reader was invited to broadcast some of these to a bedtime audience at Westfield. They were listened to attentively and a custom of transparent anonymity grew up. When the title was heard, though the name was not given till afterwards, the author, beetroot colour, scrambled down inside his bed to cover his head. Within half a second his curiosity brought him creeping up to hear his own work, leaving no one in doubt of his authorship. This recognition of good work meant much to a young author and warm were the congratulations of his fellows. NWN and CGE also instituted the 2 minute lecturettes, which the boys loved, to encourage better public speaking. The boys' command of spoken English was especially commended by inspectors, surprised at the fluency and composure of nine and ten year olds.

From an essay on trawlers: "when they want
to pull in the nets, they turn on the wenches."

Colin Eastaugh could get boys to write expressively. His neatly corrected exercise books and his own handwriting encouraged emulation. H⁺ geography lessons in the bottom form quickly became everybod·

favourite subject. His Sunday afternoon activities were meticulously planned: the eight mile hike in pairs gave a taste of freedom dependent upon acquiring skills such as map reading. Westfield, with its 50 boarders, was a brisk and happy house in the care of Colin and his wife Janet. Upon them fell innumerable duties of pastoral care and often extra chores. His splendid innovation was Music While You Wash. Loudspeakers, wired into dormitories, relayed music from the housemaster's flat. Conversation continued but boys who wanted to listen sat in dressing gowns on the front stairs. Each night was a different composer and as the works became familiar, the stairs became crowded. Friday night was Beethoven and Saturday night was pop. Rossini was a favourite and one visitor enjoyed seeing a row of 'riders' sitting up in bed urging on imaginary steeds in time to the William Tell overture. Colin had a penchant for Lambrook howlers and many in these pages were collected by him.

> *Descriptions of the model steam engine rally held in the schoolroom in January 1969 produced some lively writing: "All I could smell was methylated spirits as though I was in the grandest place in the world." "It sounded as if the engines were going to burst into tears any minute now". "Last of all there was another try at the miniature cannon. Then the fuse was lit and suddenly nothing happened."*

Cyril Ward was a keen geographer, an excellent cricket coach, and a scholarly walking encyclopedia, so wide were his interests. He was a fine musician and organist so Martyn Fothergill, in charge of music for 17 years, was glad of his help in Chapel. To the boys and his colleagues Cyril was stimulating company and he could quickly find common ground with visitors from anywhere.

> *8 year old making conversation at table:*
> *"I've got a telescope and I can see right into our neighbours' bathroom.*
> *"Do you get many surprises that way ?"*
> *"Oh no – you see we know them awfully well."*

Roger Johnson's enthusiasm so fired his young charges that they made ~at efforts, often in spare time, to research amazing topics under the of science. Both Roger and the lab were new in 1967: in 1970 came science scholarship and already the Common Entrance grades As. In an article on science teaching, he wrote of the impor- concluding: "It would be a severe deprivation if boys heir minds 'boggled' sporadically." The fives and the ed new heights with his help. He and Jane looked ll.

> Q. What does 'A bird in the hand is worth
> two in the bush' mean?
> A. One woman is worth two men.

Another who similarly fired the boys' enthusiasm was **David Backhouse** who taught junior Maths and senior games for 11 years. A colleague remarked "It's lucky David isn't keen on Shove Ha'penny or the boys would think of nothing else!"

> *Eating corn on the cob is like mowing a cylindrical lawn.*

Wing Commander **Ted Horsfall**, who played rugger for the RAF and for England, came on his retirement from the RAF. He proved to be a super coach for the top games and his gentle patience made him an admirable junior form teacher. His methodical administration and consideration endeared him to all and he was widely admired. His wife Kay helped Lambrook in many capacities. Ted's personal fitness made his sudden death from a heart attack all the more shocking to the whole community.

Don Werner, another enthusiast, was considering going full time into judo teaching in 1966 and Lambrook were lucky to collar such a gifted instructor. His judo classes for over thirty years have been enjoyed by numerous boys. Papplewick and Lambrook were the first prep schools to use his talents and have watched with admiration the reputation which his Bracknell Judo Club has achieved nationally.

> *Duty master at the end of a long day:*
> *"Haven't you got anything sensible to do ?"*
> *"Yes, Sir, I've got a very good idea but I need a*
> *penknife to do it with."*

MORE STAFF

Most masters were married and lived in the grounds. This meant babies and toddlers about the place and the boys took a proprietorial interest in the progress of teeth or talking compared with young brothers and sisters at home. Ever since 1924 when Anne was born to Guy and Marjorie Cameron, the birth of a staff baby meant a half holiday. By the 1960s half holidays, awarded for scholarships and staff babies, came thick and fast. When twins were born, the boys hoped for two half holidays and thought it a fearful swizz when only one was announced. The father of the twins had a squint and a junior wag commented "Bit of luck he had two babies – he'd have seen two anyway!"

The boys' gardens flooded one wet May: "It took all the half holiday to bail our garden out. First the rosebush came in sight and then, after hours more, we came to the pansies."
QUERY: where did they put all that water if not into the next garden?

A wonderful bonus was the help of masters' wives in the matrons' department, nursing, escorting boys to appointments and sometimes airports, preparing for a special occasion or simply coping in a crisis. Even a routine dental appointment for a boy who lived abroad complicated matters if another boy needed an emergency X-ray on the same day or on a match day already busy with visitors and team clothes, or on Sister's day off when the HM's wife stood in for her. Mrs.Forbes often filled gaps but when gaps occurred simultaneously it was impossible to cover them without those skilled and kindly part time helpers. They were friends of boys and staff and no community can have too many friends.

A 15 year old wrote about his plans: he wanted to read medicine and work for the World Health Organisation, adding "I hope I shan't have got married by then but I am afraid I may, which will rather muck things up."

Edythe Jamieson spent two years as housekeeper, or, as she put it, Mrs. Forbes' apprentice, and returned in 1967 as Domestic Bursar responsible for almost everything. What a whirlwind of Scots fun she was, cooking with one hand, teaching others to cook, planning a party (it was never long between parties) persuading domestic staff of various nationalities to agree with each other, and naming two new dishwashers Colin and Hamish after two Lambrook boys who helped in an emergency. Edythe enjoyed boys' requests like "Please may we have some jelly for bacteria to eat ?" before a science experiment and the nickname given to her chocolate crisp pudding, served with chocolate sauce one really wet winter: "Pickaxe pud with Sixth game rugger ground".

Mrs.Rush was a tiny person of uncertain years and unfailingly serene – a blessing in a community. Her cars became a legend. She traded them regularly in the pre M.O.T.days and car enthusiasts on the staff were amazed that she got such old bangers to go. Tuesday was her day off and we all came eagerly to elevenses next day to hear about the latest breakdown or lift back. One car had the driver's door lock jammed which would not have mattered much if the passenger door had worked but that too was faulty. For months she used the rear door, climbing over into the driver's seat. Another car seized up when she forgot to remove the red rug she had put under the bonnet. It started but quickly suffocated and strips of red rug emerged for a long time. She was wonderfully unruffled through these adventures and enjoyed relating them.

> *A letter from a 13 year old said "At prep school I used to love fooling around but here it is not so much fun because it's easy to do and nobody ever catches you".*

The matrons turned their hands to anything, sorting and mending clothes, inspecting ears and toes and fingernails at bathtime, answering a thousand queries. A dozen named jars lived on the workroom mantelpiece so that boys could deposit dental plates in safety and be reminded to collect them after games. When dyslexia first raised its head but before it became constant enough to require special remedial help, several boys trotted to the workroom with their reading books and gained confidence from these patient and humorous young women in white.

> *The Angles, Saxons and the Jutes crossed the sea in open boots.*

The school nurse is rather like a racing car mechanic, ready at the pits for repairs but hopeful of getting a car back on the track soon. In an ideal world a new nurse would have no one ill for the first few weeks while she got to know the community and and observed a flock of lively children. They must learn that she is interested in them when they are well and active, not just when they are ill. Sister's surgery queue always held surprises and I enjoyed my weekly duty on her day off. A few boys obviously came for entertainment, because they wanted a one to one conversation. Amid the hurly burly of school life, more people talk than listen. Keen games players might be reluctant to report something which could put them on the Off Games list. Others, facing a daunting task, might need reassurance. Few needed pills and potions but all needed a welcome. We had some fine nurses who won everybody's confidence.

> *Once a boy rushed out of Chapel, handkerchief to mouth but was comprehensively sick in the doorway. The congregation were already singing the last hymn so those at the front missed Sister's white starched long jump as she trotted out to take the unfortunate to a Higher Place. With books and heads held high the choir were unaware of the horror that awaited them as they processed towards the door. Mrs.Forbes galloped out, jumped the hazard and, seizing the vast square doormat from the passage, dropped it like Sir Walter's cloak at the feet of the advancing Christian soldiers who emerged as triumphantly dry shod as the Israelites crossing the Red Sea.*

ICE
HOCKEY
MATCH,
1962

*on
St. Ronan's
lake next
door.*

Occasionally, if a boy retired to the sickroom, parents coming to take him out for the day were asked to postpone their visit – a task I hated. Salvation appeared in the guise of a nurse, meticulous at her job but tricky for anyone to get on with, who enjoyed imparting bad news. As she told me of little Willy's high temperature and his need to spend the day in bed, she would rub her hands with glee, asking eagerly "Shall I telephone his parents ? I can tell them: I'll do it !" A plump nurse whose name was Carter was swiftly nicknamed Magna. Another asked a boy when he got headaches and his reply was "Mostly in Latin!"

One evening a theatre party was arranged for several staff and it left us shorthanded at bedtime, where, for the fifty youngest boys, we usually had Sister upstairs, a matron in the boys' bathroom and another roaming around the dormitories. In boys' tea Philip asked for the boys' cooperation as a new nurse was helping temporarily. After evening Chapel, he dashed upstairs to be disguised in an overall with white cap and apron and was ready to take Sister's queue. Gigantic bottles of coloured water and big serving spoons were in the cupboard. The queue should have been a mere half dozen boys but the first comers were so intrigued by the gruff voice and ladles of weird medicine that word spread quickly and the queue stretched down two flights of stairs. Boys in high spirits were not sure if this was a real new nurse to whom they must at all costs be polite. One young Sherlock suspected 'her' feet were too big. The boys had a merry evening, the duty master had a half empty play hour, I collared the two boys who needed regular medication and the real matrons enjoyed the theatre.

During the great freeze up of 1962, the boys skated on the lake next door and ice hockey matches were played against Ludgrove and St. George's, Windsor. Lambrook's team, dressed alike in corduroy trousers, green jerseys and bobble caps included the headmaster's daughter Alison, who was the first Lambrook girl. One boy in the Lambrook team had fair curls which convinced St. George's that he was the girl whom they must massacre at all costs. As the whole opposition team tackled him, the unmarked Lambrook players won convincingly.

It is sad not to record the names and deeds of innumerable ancillary staff whose presence encouraged us all and whose work enabled the community to run smoothly – most of the time anyway. Dorothy Williams, confidant of three generations, worked with a smile for 27 years above and below stairs. She was loved and trusted by everyone.

Philip had always intended becoming a parish priest again for the last years of his ministry. In July 1970 he gave notice to the governors, of whom he was then chairman, that they should look for a new headmaster for September 1971. Parishes usually do not look for a new vicar more than six months ahead, so the Brownless family did not know for several months where they would be next year. When eventually the applications from prospective headmasters for Lambrook were sorted out, and several parishes had interviewed Philip, 1971 was several months old. The summer term sped by faster than ever with the new headmaster and his wife coming several times to meet everyone at Lambrook and the Hampshire parish waiting for Philip's arrival in September.

A DIGRESSION ON
PAST MASTERS

TWO MASTERS IN THE 1920s resented the fact that the owner of Westfield seldom used his full sized billiard table. They used to creep through the hedge in the wee small hours, break into his billiard room, play their game in silence and creep out undetected.

* * * * * * *

The masters in the 1930s were fed up with the piece of cheese which kept appearing for their supper so they buried it in the flower pot holding the fern on the long dining table. The fern thrived and the smell ripened wonderfully but the source could not be traced. The masters kept quiet till the floorboards were to be investigated and then went in a sheepish body to own up.

* * * * * * *

Another master had too many flutters on the gee gees. The debt came to the headmaster's ears so the man was carpeted, the debt paid from an advance of salary and thereafter for several terms he went weekly meekly to the study for his tiny pocket money allowance. He was a good teacher but of the sort Ian Hay described as "a man among boys and a boy among men."

* * * * * * *

When myxamatosis was rife, there were two masters with somewhat crumpled faces. The sleepier of the two came into the Common room laughing one day which was so unusual that everyone looked up. He said "It's the funniest thing I've ever heard – do you know what the boys call Blank ?" (referring to his crumple faced colleague.) "They call him Mixy Bunny!" The other masters spluttered into their elevenses having known for months past that this man's nickname was 'Mixy Minor".

* * * * * * *

The staff did a pantomime for the boys one Christmas. Mr. X fancied himself as a smooth mover and volunteered for a solo dance spot. He wore a slinky blue evening gown with narrow straps over his swanlike shoulders and did some vaguely swanlike movements to some vaguely swanlike music. His colleagues knew he had thoroughly enjoyed preparing all this but the boys were very sorry for him and said how awful it was for poor Mr. X having to do that awful dance. Awfully bad luck.

* * * * * * *

Another entertainment culminated in a gipsy feast. Philip as the gipsy hunter was to fire a gun in the playground and enter carrying a pheasant (actually some socks) for the cooking pot: on the night he went one better and carried in the elderly corpse of a pigeon which had been hanging in the vegetable garden. The Gipsy Queen's pleasure became a shriek of disgust as she dropped it into the pot. R.V. Johns as the Gipsy King had long since despaired of learning his lines and wrote them with a mapping pen on a scrap of paper stuck on his tobacco tin. This seemed a brilliant solution until the producer said the Gipsy King must not wear spectacles. The common gypsies mutinied till the King was granted a special dispensation. Success now seemed within reach but no – it was so dark without the overhead lights that RVJ could hardly see the campfire, let alone read his crib. It was a line that everyone else found easy, about the gorillas to be found in the jungles of Burma – a play on the nicknames of Philip and RVJ himself but no prompting helped. He should have swaggered centre stage as the genial host but he crouched down to read by the footlights with his back to the audience who had no idea what he was doing and could not hear a word he said. However, the boys knew a comedy when they saw one and laughed till they were exhausted.

* * * * * *

There was once a master Who Shall Be Nameless. He was a shocking driver and those who accepted a lift in his open tourer only did so once. When he said he was taking his mother on a motor tour of Scotland in August there was much ribaldry and the common room joker said it would undoubtedly kill the old girl. When the masters assembled next term word reached them – luckily just before he did – that his mother had died on the trip. This was just the sort of joke they appreciated and the bearer of the sad tidings had difficulty quelling their mirth before the man appeared. It was true. His mother, well wrapped up in rugs at his side, had become silent and when he took another glance after more hairpin bends and precipices, he saw that she had indeed died. The nearest help was fifteen miles away through ever wilder glens and when he reached the tiny police station the explanations proved to be another marathon.

* * * * * *

There was once a young fair haired master who looked even younger than his years. Naughty boys loved to make him blush and would ask "Sir, what are you going to do, Sir, when you leave school, Sir?"

* * * * * *

MARRIAGES

The following met at Lambrook, were married and lived happily ever after:

The Bentleys	- she came twice to nurse in epidemics.
The Camerons	- she was the headmaster's daughter.
The Chittendons	- she was a matron.
The Crawshaws	- she was junior mistress.
The Galsworthys	- she was a matron.
The Hunts	- she was the headmaster's secretary.
The Rankins	- she was a matron.

Privacy is scarce in a community : one of these men proposed in the bus going to Windsor (after parrying questions from nosy boys) and another in a quiet lane nearby (two bicycles were spotted leaning against each other in a gateway). Yet another popped the question in the linen cupboard. Enough said.

* * * * * *

JACQUELINE
AND
TOM CLOUGH
1989

THE SCHOOLROOM

*Built in 1888 it has held plays, concerts, debates, services and much
else. Here are some of the old desks with china inkwells. In 1973 the
schoolroom was widened to become the dininghall.*

7

T.V.CLOUGH
HEADMASTER
1971–1989

THE NEW HEADMASTER, THOMAS VERNON CLOUGH, and his wife Jacqueline arrived at Lambrook with their three school age children in the hot August of 1971. Tom was an energetic man of 42, with a Cambridge degree in modern languages, who had represented his college at rugger, sailing and athletics. Jacqueline trained at Atholl Crescent and the Edinburgh College of Art and her delightful young presence prompted one boy to describe her approvingly to his mother as a "real bird". Tom had taught in both prep and public schools and they came from a successful housemastership at Blundells. In a twinkling, it seemed, they got to know Lambrook boys, staff, parents, the place and dozens of Old Boys. They were school minded and family minded in the best sense.

Tom took on what he himself described as a tight ship, with an excellent staff and a full entry list for several years ahead as Philip had been booking prospective pupils even in his last term. It soon became apparent that the Cloughs' ideas for modernising aspects of the school would take effect gently. Perhaps this reassured the boy who had asked Philip "What will happen to the Chapel when you go, Sir?" The Cloughs shared a lively Christian faith and the care of each individual was as important as ever. The Family Service which he introduced attracted crowds of parents. When we stayed to supper after Philip had preached in Chapel, we admired the courtesy with which they answered incessant knocks at the door and telephone enquiries throughout the evening after a fourteen hour day. Also admirable was the speed with which they had got to know Lambrook's neighbours and their hope that Lambrook itself would be a good neighbour to the village. It did so in several new ways: the new swimming bath was appreciated by a group of local people and soon, as a result of Roger Johnson's local interest, a group of boys as 'social service' were helping nearby pensioners with their gardens. Jacqueline was very good to those who, though new to her, were old friends of the school.

Perhaps *The Chronicle* was the first evidence of new management. Virtually unchanged for seventy years, it had begun to look dowdy. Tom kept the dark green cover but now with photographs and reproductions of boys' art work, plus updated typography, it was rejuvenated. Three generations of the Butcher family's printing firm in Ascot had overseen its production: now the latest Mr.Butcher gently modernised it.

Long laid plans for reordering the buildings came to fruition soon after Tom's arrival. When the assembly hall adjoining the Chapel and the new classroom block (making the playground a quadrangle) were completed in 1973, the old schoolroom became the dininghall connected to the rejuvenated kitchens. No longer would food be prepared on one floor and eaten on the floor above! The old dininghall became the library: the east end of the dininghall was separated off and the school office returned to this room, close to the front door, where it had been till 1930. The old IA and ID became a new art room and orchestra room respectively.

What a wealth of dust and turmoil are concealed in those few lines! There was plenty more of both to come for the Cloughs. Several appeals were mounted and

PHOTOGRAPH BY COURTESY OF ROGER SMEETON 1997

the *Chronicles* give only an inkling in a few euphemistic lines of the mess, noise and upheaval endured not only by those who worked at Lambrook in termtime but – far worse – by those who lived there during the holidays.

1978   An appeal raised money for the building of a proper art room and an all weather pitch (hockey, basket ball, tennis etc.) at last reducing the school's dependence upon muddy fields. Art teaching throughout the school took on a new dimension under Jacqueline's guidance and a proper studio was needed since all forms now worked in clay and other media on a weekly basis.

1981   A staircase was built to connect the private side bedrooms with the Cloughs' new dining room on the ground floor.

1983   New school WC block was built. A squash court was built. The old recreation room was converted to accommodate computers and this extra subject was somehow shoe horned into the timetable.

1984   A new teaching block was built near the squash court, to contain senior classrooms and specialist teaching rooms. The top floor of the old classroom block became the science teaching area: the lower floor and Remove landing became the music teaching and practice area, with the former IB becoming a Music room and the former Remove a video lecture theatre. This appeal was headed by a professional organiser who became ill half way. Tom undertook the additional work himself.

THE ART ROOM
A display on Parent's Day

With this lot triumphantly completed in 1985, the Governors and Tom hoped for a peaceful year with only the front of Lambrook to be painted. After five weeks' snow, the scaffolding went up in March 1986 but the old render beneath the painted plaster was found to be faulty and every bit had to be sandblasted back to the original brick. The work was not finished until September 1987. Living inside, while the building was drilled and hammered and blasted, was grim indeed with dust everywhere.

In 1988 Westfield had to be re-roofed. It is possible that the Cloughs began to think of Tom's 60 th birthday the following year and that retiring to a house of their own might be pleasant.

ACTIVITIES AND OUTINGS

Visitors to Lambrook in the Cloughs' time were impressed by lively boys who gladly talked of their various activities. With art and music playing a prominent part in the lives of everyone, not just a few, the scope of Lambrook's interests increased. Educational visits and outings, rare earlier, became more frequent in the '80s with the acquisition of a school minibus. The Science Museum and the National Gallery were obvious destinations but groups also went to plays, concerts and exhibitions at nearby schools, to a factory, a vineyard, a sheep farm, the police dog training centre, the Royal Mews and much more. Geography field trips became regular events, sometimes involving a night at a youth hostel. Only the dormitory captains had an outing formerly: now the leavers were treated to a camp away for several days. The windband too made regular sorties to play elsewhere. Other schools were all doing outings and expeditions in the affluent eighties. It meant extra work for the staff but enlivened school wonderfully for the boys. The Westfield Fete, Roger Johnson's initiative, became a popular fund raising event for charity each summer.

NEW MEMBERS OF STAFF

When senior posts fell vacant, Tom found able and experienced men: Robin Gilkes, 1976 to 1997, took English and history for the top forms and coached the first game cricket and soccer. Andrew Brown arrived in 1979 to take the senior classics and became Westfield's housemaster. Ian Stewart, 1981 to 1997, ran the French department and top games. Tom asked Ben Brownless to fill a three weeks' teaching gap one summer and offered him a job when he graduated in 1980. After seven years Ben left to gain experience elsewhere but returned three years later to run the geography and build up the new department of Design Technology under the next headmaster in 1990. Several people have served twice on the Lambrook staff but three times is unique! Tom often employed a 'student prince' temporarily and some of these youngsters developed a taste for teaching, almost to their own surprise. Peter Hopkins, who came in 1983 to teach middle school subjects, made a unique contribution: his forte was magic and he imparted skills to boys whose presentation and dexterity have won high praise from professionals. In addition to the Magic Shows, he produced a series of fine school plays.

GOODBYE AND THANK YOU

Peter Granger, Chairman of Governors, summed up the Cloughs' time thus: "Eighteen years is a long time to be in the same job but their enthusiasm never waned. In 1971 there were 120 boys at Lambrook – now there are 140. The outstanding scholastic record has been maintained: in 1977 there were seven scholarships. In games, the record is also good, with the undefeated cricket team of 1984, the all conquering rugger team of 1987 and the winning of the Prep Schools Rugby Fives championship in the same year being noteworthy. It is a pleasure to be greeted by a Lambrook boy as they are so well mannered.

It is through these achievements and providing a well balanced education for all boys that Lambrook has kept its record as one of the leading boarding preparatory schools for boys."

A DIGRESSION ON JOURNEYS

EVEN IF FRIENDS AND ACTIVITIES at school are enjoyable, the journey there is usually felt as dreary, even grim. For two boys in 1879 it must have seemed endless: their headmaster had spent part of the holidays close to their grandmother's house and they travelled back to school with him.

These two were the young Prince Christian Victor and Prince Albert Victor, staying with Mr. and Mrs. Burnside at Birchwood Cottage, near Balmoral. Their journey was recorded in the Court Circular and Mr. Burnside probably enjoyed pasting these cuttings into his scrapbook with Sir Henry Ponsonby's telegram expressing "Her Majesty's relief at hearing of the young Princes' safe arrival back at school."

The London and South Western Railway reached Bracknell and Wokingham in 1875.

When the five Gray brothers were at Lambrook in 1900 most boys travelled to and from school by train. Sergeant Major Butt arranged the transport to Bracknell Station, bought their tickets and saw them into the right trains. 'Hay wagons were provided by a local farmer. Each wagon was drawn by two carthorses which seldom even trotted. The boys sat on benches along the sides of the wagon and much time was spent over the journey.'

When Cuthbert Norris Elye travelled by train in 1902 his ticket from Lowth to London cost 11 shillings and threepence (about £31 today). At Kings Cross his aunt met him and took him back to her house in Courtfield Gardens. Actually his aunt waited in her carriage with its pair of horses while her footman met CLNE on the platform and tipped the porter sixpence for seeing to the luggage. After lunch he was driven back to Waterloo and put into the charge of the duty master for the train journey to Bracknell.

Christopher Hanbury, (1914–1918) lived near Burnham, Bucks. "I was always conveyed to and from Lambrook in a dogcart driven by our old groom. He was an unforthcoming character and our journeys to school were pretty lugubrious. On the way home I prattled away merrily but I don't think he had any idea what I was talking about."

During the 1920s and 1930s cars increased till only about half the boys travelled by train. A tradition of cheerful rivalry grew between trainboys and carboys, known as 'Car slops.' The last day of term was called payday as pocket money, banked during termtime, was given back. The carboys, Sunday suited after their payday baths (every boy had a bath on the last day) and sternly bidden to keep clean, watched enviously as the train boys, due to bath at bedtime, enjoyed riotous activities. The car boys left that afternoon and the camaraderie increased as the numbers dwindled. Next morning on Bracknell Station a new rivalry sprang up. The Waterloo train left two minutes ahead of the Reading train so the Waterloo boys, city bound, used to call across the tracks "Reading pigs – see them off to market," to which came the ritual reply: "Waterloo slops – can't wait to see your mummies!"

At this time Lambrook drew boys from all over the UK. There were a few Scots, a Yorkshire contingent, about ten for Bristol, several for East Anglia and a west country group who travelled together to Exeter where parents met them for even further onward journeys. Even into the 1960s, the next generation of these far flung faithful families still sent sons to Lambrook but by then the attractions of schools nearer home had increased and many railway lines had been closed.

* * * * * * *

The most adventurous journeys were undertaken by Sir Roy Redgrave (1935-1939) who then lived in Roumania and later wrote this account for his grandchildren.

"I was put on the train in the care of three of my mother's fussing friends who clucked all the way to England. Campina railway station was three days and three nights from Victoria station, whatever route was taken, the Nord express via Berlin, the Orient Express via Vienna or the Simplon Express via Zagreb. The last adult entrusted with putting me on the school train at Waterloo was Uncle George, making his first visit to England.

In the event it was I who guided him through the ferry, Customs and immigration procedures and finally to London. Next morning I sat in the Regent Palace Hotel watching with growing admiration as Uncle George attacked his first English breakfast. Grapefruit, prunes, porridge and kippers were soon dispatched. The waiter did not bat an eyelid when he proceeded to order kidneys, eggs, sausages, bacon and mushrooms. I realised nothing was going to stop him until he had tried everything on the menu, finishing as an afterthought with American waffles and syrup. We then rushed around London sightseeing in a most haphazard manner, into red double decker buses, down into the underground, into taxis and on one memorable occasion down into the ladies' lavatory in Leicester Square. We had lunch at Simpsons and tea at Gunters and then hurried to Waterloo station just in time for me to catch the five o'clock school train to Bracknell.

After my trip with Uncle George I was allowed to travel alone. My father took the attendant aside, gave him a tip and asked him to keep an eye on his nine year old son but it soon became evident that he had other things to do. My first trip started well: at each stop I lowered the window to watch the milling crowds, the fresh walnut and yogurt vendors and the engineer tapping the wheels with a long handled hammer. The dining car attendant announced first and second service and was followed by a column of my fellow passengers. But here was something for which I was totally unprepared – it was impossible to enter that awesome dining car alone, to select a table, to sit opposite a stranger and then to read a menu. For the next day or so I eked out a packet of biscuits and two bars of chocolate which my grandmother had slipped into my bag. By lunchtime on the third day I was feeling very hungry and sorry for myself as the now familiar line of passengers passed along the corridor. Suddenly the door slid open and a lady said "Do excuse me, but would you like to accompany me ? I do so hate eating alone." I leapt to my feet and followed. She was something to do with Missions to Seamen and had guessed my predicament. The waiter saw that I had not used any of my meal coupons and gave me generous helpings. That lady became my idol, a dream in pale blue and she completely restored my self confidence.

One of the hazards of travelling alone was that I never knew with whom I might have to share the compartment. In 1936 an enormous Turk got on at Berlin. All my life I had been brought up to fear the Turks. They had skinned an ancestor alive in 1714, my grandfather had fought them in Bulgaria in 1877 and my father had been wounded by them in Palestine in 1917. They had massacred Greeks and Armenians just before I was born and I was now terrified. Poor man, he tried so hard to be friendly, showing me a huge box of cigars which he hoped to take through Customs, a wooden box with six cut throat razors and a book of photographs of the Olympic Games in Berlin. Perhaps he was a weight lifter. Anyway I lay in the bottom bunk too scared to disturb him, let alone use the remarkable china sauceboat stored beneath the washbasin. Long after dawn I was still motionless, longing to lift the blind and see where we were. Eventually the attendant looked in and told me the Turk had been taken off the train in the night by Customs officers. I heaved a huge sigh of relief and dived for the receptacle under the washstand.

I estimate that I spent between two and three weeks on the train each year and had less holidays than any boy at school. Europe was becoming a suspicious and dangerous place as more countries came under Nazi domination. Whereas only Turkey had required a passport in 1876, now every country imposed its Customs and immigration controls. There was always tension as officials in an array of different uniforms tramped through the train at every frontier crossing. My letters home began to contain descriptions of searches for Jews, of people being taken off the train, of black uniforms and jack boots. The journey was no longer fun."

* * * * * * *

A master on duty accompanied the school trains from Waterloo and Reading and school caps identified the various groups assembling on the platform. Colonel Dudley Michell (1906–1911) saw his nephews on to the school train in the 1960s and then wrote to the Headmaster "Heatherdown were on the same platform at Waterloo: my trigger finger itched!"

World War Two brought petrol rationing. Parents shared transport and a variety of vehicles used to disgorge boys and school trunks. A pony and trap appeared. Train journeys were often disrupted and took so long that boys arrived at school tired, hungry and dirty.

In the late 1950s one or two forces' children began to travel by air arriving at odd times. His headmaster, Philip Brownless, remembers chatting with Alistair Irwin at midnight while he turned out his flightbag to find various papers to hand over for safe keeping. Philip's war had taken him across the world but this ten year old's logbook showed many more strange places than his headmaster had seen. A late arrival went into the sickbay so he could sleep till he wanted to wake. Daytime arrivals went into school but once they had claimed their lockers and greeted their friends, they were invited to the sickroom to sleep the clock round. The word jetlag was not yet current.

In 1960, 4 or 5 boys travelled to and fro by air. By 1970 this had doubled. These were children of diplomats, of service personnel, or of businessmen working abroad. Not all these boys flew overseas every holidays. From then on the number increased steeply, posing a tremendous extra load on the secretary, the workroom who had to get them ready at strange times and on staff charged with airport duties. Meeting one child at London Airport may be time consuming: imagine the complications for two masters with one minibus of meeting a dozen boys arriving separately at all four terminals on the same evening! The school secretary wrestles with considerable logistical problems.

James Torrie was 11 when he wrote about "My favourite place" and chose Fleet Station. He described it with delight: it was for him a symbol of all the joy of homecoming "because then I know I am back in happy Hampshire".

HOW FAR AWAY FROM LAMBROOK DID THE BOYS LIVE ?

	Less than 20 miles	More than 100 miles	Abroad
c 1885	12 %	29 %	Approx 5 %
c 1910	6 %	19 %	Approx 4 %
c 1920	37 %	22 %	Approx 3 %
c 1930	47 %	18 %	Approx 10 %

Parents living abroad during these years probably only saw their sons for one holiday a year, if that. The following figures indicate regular air travel.

	Less than 20 miles	More than 100 miles	Abroad
c 1950	42 %	14 %	6 %
c 1970	34 %	16 %	10 %
c 1980	58 %	3 %	25 %
c 1990	34 %	2 %	27 %

INDEPENDENT SCHOOLS
IN THE 1980s

MORE PUPILS AND BIGGER BUILDINGS seemed to be the trend of the
'80s. Every school increased its numbers. By the end of the decade
many had opened pre preparatory departments as 'feeders' to the
main school. Co education was clearly sensible at ages 4 to 8 so why not
at the prepschool stage as well, argued those schools who wanted to keep
their extra spaces filled. Certainly the one stop school (both sexes and a
wide age range) was more attractive to busy parents than daily trips to
several schools. This made the girls' schools feel vulnerable: many of the
boys' public schools were accepting girls into their VI forms, from altruis-
tic motives they said, though the girls' schools felt that finance and university results might have something to do with it.

While the national total of pupils in the private sector increased during
the 1980s, the number of boarders showed a steady decline, particularly
at prep school age.

Market forces now held sway and a whole new schools' marketing
industry came into being. ISIS, the Independent Schools Information
Service, did a good job in raising public awareness of independent education as well as providing first aid to schools who found themselves belea-
guered for whatever reason.

The Thatcher years bred a generation who questioned authority, who
would buy an education for their children if convinced it was good but
who wanted their young at home at night. The salaried mother, who knew
what she wanted and could pay for it, was no longer a rare bird.

Lambrook had a glorious site but, and it was a big BUT, plenty of
schools had found the Thames Valley a good catchment area. There were
now too many schools chasing too few pupils and parents knew it. They
were spoilt for choice: early booking and waiting lists were things of the
far past.

Education having become an easily purchased commodity, dissatisfied
parents could chop and change in a way unimaginable earlier. In the
1950s, a boy just might be removed to a crammer for his last couple of
terms but it was almost unheard of for him to go to another prep school. A
strict headmasterly etiquette was observed in such a case and the two
headmasters delicately discussed whether due notice had been given and
if there were any debts outstanding at School One. It was to School Two's
benefit not to get landed with a bad payer or feckless parents. During the

1980s, this etiquette began to melt: from circling and sniffing, dog came nearer to eating dog. Boys did occasionally leave Lambrook early to go to another prepschool and – an omen of the times – Lambrook was able to accept late arrivals who had had a year or two elsewhere. An empty bed was uneconomic but late arrivals, by altering the age balance of the school, had a disproportionate effect delayed by two or three years. Then it could mean a huge leave, which could not be fully replaced by new boys.

The day of the all male, all boarding prep school was drawing to a close. Schools were facing new demands and it was up to heads and governors to decide which changes were ephemeral and which must be taken seriously. In addition to opening pre prep departments, some boarding prep schools were already taking day children. This decision, which may have appeared less momentous than taking girls, was probably the one whose ripple effects changed the schools most.

The recession, beginning in 1989, had grim effects in all schools. All parents felt financially uncertain and some were made redundant. Lambrook had up to 30% of service children, many of whose fees were subsidised by the Ministry of Defence: splendid children and splendid families but when the M.O.D. had to cut these allowances, Lambrook caught a cold rather than a sneeze. Many schools caught colds and worse: there were closures and mergers on all sides and the Thames Valley saw its share. Governing bodies wrestled with interlocking problems.

LAMBROOK
Aerial photograph of the school by John Keeling 1991.

LAMBROOK SCHOOL 1997

130

Ryan
Hewitt

Marilyn
Hawes

Claire   Helen   John   Liesbeth   Sheena   Susan   Gareth   Andrew   Robin   Angela   Robin   Ben   Ian   Peter   Stuart   Dominic   Beth   Lyn   Sarah   Isabel   Sara
Adriaansen   Wells   Greatrix   Gunter   Stewart   Carter   Barnes   Browne   Gilkes   Badham   Badham   Brownless Stewart   Hopkins   Hartley   Price   Higgins   Churcher   Tysoe   Lethbridge Stevens
                                                                                                        Thornhill   Thornhill   Thornhill   Joanna
   Wattis

PHOTOGRAPH BY COURTESY OF GILLMAN & SOAME

9

LAMBROOK
IN THE 1990s

W HEN THE GOVERNORS CAME TO APPOINT a new headmaster in 1989, Michael C. Bickersteth, an Old Boy, was a likely candidate. He had been second in command elsewhere, they had a young family and his wife, Sally, already had experience as a matron in a boarding school. They seemed admirably qualified and were a very nice couple.

1989 was not an easy time to become a headmaster at Lambrook or anywhere else. External pressures on heads and staff at all schools were increasing. The Children Act and inspections by Social Services and by the Independent Schools Joint Council involved mountains of paperwork on the headmaster's desk. The requirements were not difficult for a school like Lambrook to comply with but all needed planning and describing: only a few (like siting a telephone for the children's use and coping with the attendant complications of mislaid phone cards!) proved awkward. The regulations of the Health and Safety at Work Act, new Food Handling regulations, plus endless changes to the National Curriculum were all implemented during these few years.

Michael Bickersteth may have expected Lambrook to be rather as he remembered it: the Governors' expectations may have been different. The headmaster and the staff suddenly had a mass of new legislation to cope with on top of running a school. They were hard pressed. MCB saw a new support structure as needed (the Children Act had already required some formalisation of pastoral care) and appointed Ben Brownless as Deputy Head and Andrew Brown as Director of Studies. On the bricks and mortar side, MCB saw two needs: a department for Design Technology, already part of the National Curriculum, and a sports hall, the gymnasium having become the DT department. These differing expectations seem to be the probable cause of the malaise which came upon the place. MCB's cautious diffidence may have appeared as indecision and communication with parents was not always easy. Numbers began to drop, aggravated by three huge leaves. At the end of summer term 1992 the Bickersteths left, dignified to the very end.

Ian and Sheena Stewart were asked by the Governors to run Lambrook for two terms. They did very well – two safe pairs of hands. They showed round prospectives and booked some – no mean feat when everything was so uncertain. To their credit, it was to Lambrook that a welcome influx of boys came when a nearby school fell on hard times.

The Governors' first task was to appoint a new headmaster. They were already busy with the last stages of the fund raising and building of the Sports Hall which opened in November 1992. Now plans for a Pre Prep department were urgently discussed: Ben Brownless drew up plans and detailed costings for this, as well as a marketing plan for Lambrook which soon proved its worth by increasing local interest. Peter Granger, Chairman of Governors since 1981, has been a level headed adviser, working untiringly for Lambrook behind the scenes.

In April 1993 Robin Badham Thornhill and his wife Angela arrived at Lambrook with their two daughters. He was 36 and they had run a very successful house at Cheltenham. He worked unstintingly to stabilise Lambrook's position but his achievements cannot yet be described in detail. *Mirabile dictu*, he succeeded in reversing the downward trend: in four years his decisive mind and easy manner coped with more than many headmasters meet in 40 years. He became headmaster of Summer Fields, Oxford, in September 1997.

Another success story is that of the Lambrook Pre Prep department, housed in the fine rooms at Westfield, for children of 4½ to 8. They trot round purposefully taking French and computing in their stride. In September 1993 it had four children and in September 1997 it had grown to 69. Sheena Stewart, the head, has assembled an admirable staff and has implemented all the hopes invested in it. The Pre Prep use the Lambrook swimming pool and the sports hall and go over to an early sitting for lunch in the dininghall. Best of all, the children enjoy a huge lawn and the grounds for play.

LAMBROOK HAILEYBURY

Several months had been filled with secret plans, confidential negotiations, clandestine meetings and even after dark assignations in country pubs. A full account must wait for the pen of one of those involved: the present writer can only sketch an outline.

Robin Badham Thornhill's appointment to Summer Fields was announced in November 1996 to the disappointment of those who hoped he would reap what he and his team had so diligently sown.

The Lambrook Governors – possibly with a sigh – advertised for yet another new headmaster, little knowing that (in another part of the forest) the Governors of Haileybury Junior School in Windsor were worried about the limitations of their site, which was neither secure nor big enough for their needs.

For some months, talk of mergers had been conducted amid deep security between headmasters and governors of various schools, all anxious that nothing should leak to a rival. When John Hare, headmaster of Haileybury, put the idea to his Governors of a merger with Lambrook, and applied to the Governors of Lambrook as a candidate for Lambrook's vacant headship, it seemed the pieces of the jigsaw were slotting wonderfully into place.

Of the schools in the area, Haileybury's ethos, boys and parents are most like Lambrook's, says one who knows both schools well. The merger is seen as a partnership not a take over of one school by another. Haileybury moved to the Lambrook site in September 1997 with John Hare as headmaster of the new combined school.

The equation which suggested 80 boys was the right number for an all boarding prep school in the 1930s and 100 in the 1950s now gives a figure of around 200 children for a largely day prepschool with a pre prep department. Only with this number can the school attract and afford the good staff on which it depends. More staff are needed today than in former times. The nationwide change from an authoritarian discipline to a more relaxed approach requires more supervision of children. Costs increase as all schools provide more facilities and activities. Slide rules cannot compete with computers.

This account of the recent past ends on an up beat: the future pupils of the combined school, though it will be a new one in some ways (and a good thing too, say those who never sat on a soft seat during their Lambrook time) have the traditions of both schools to look back on and a bright future in front of them.

PHOTOGRAPH BY COURTESY OF JOHN KEELING 1991

POSTSCRIPT

Commander P.B. Jackson R.N. had not known Lambrook before he came to run the appeal in 1978. Afterwards he wrote:

> *"One cannot overstress the warmth of feeling that Lambrook has engendered during its long period as a preparatory school through a great many generations of Old Boys, very many of whom have sent their own sons through the school.*
>
> *Parents are convinced that Lambrook produces and develops the best in their sons, and none of those seen had the slightest misgivings regarding any aspect of the school or staff; in fact the feeling gained is that of a large family gathering, which succeeds in developing a well adjusted and educated teenager who can look forward to a happy future."*

This book began with a remark from a boy which could have been uttered in any decade between 1860 and 1997. The last word is a similarly timeless remark: a 13 year old writing from his next school to thank the Lambrook staff ended his letter:

> *"Thank you very much for all the time*
> *and trouble you gave for me.*
> *I appreciate it much more now."*